THE CLASSIC TREK CREW BOOK

JAMES VAN HISE

Photo on title page: March 28, 1978 as the cast of STAR TREK: THE MOTION PICTURE appear at a press conference. Left to Right: DeForest Kelley, Nichelle Nichols, Leonard Nimoy, William Shatner, Persis Khambatta, Walter Koenig, Grace Lee Whitney and James Doohan. © 1978 Ron Galella Ltd.

Library of Congress Cataloging-in-Publication Data
James Van Hise

The Classic Trek Crew Book

1. The Classic Trek Crew Book (television, popular culture)
I. Title

Published by Pioneer Books, Inc., 5715 N. Balsam Rd., Las Vegas, NV, 89130.

First Printing, 1993

For All Those Who Dream Of Better Times & Better Places.

ક્ષ ક્ષ

JAMES VAN HISE writes about film, television and comic book history. He has written numerous books on these subjects, including BATMANIA, TREK: THE NEXT GENERATION, THE TREK CREW BOOK, STEPHEN KING & CLIVE BARKER: THE ILLUSTRATED GUIDE TO THE MASTERS OF THE MACABRE and HOW TO DRAW ART FOR COMIC BOOKS: LESSONS FROM THE MASTERS. He is the publisher of MIDNIGHT GRAFFITI, in which he has run previously unpublished stories by Stephen King and Harlan Ellison. Van Hise resides in San Diego along with his wife, horses and various other animals.

Publisher and Designer: Hal Schuster   *Editor: David Lessnick*

CONTENTS

FOREWORDS

Why are you reading this book? Why is STAR TREK still so popular after all these years? Let's discuss the reasons why....

CLASSIC TREK—
FOUNDATIONS OF THE FUTURE

When STAR TREK premiered in 1966, the Space Race was going full steam, but the dream of reaching beyond the mortal confines of our world seemed like just that—a dream. Add to this the fact that America was plunging deeper into the morass of Southeast Asia and the future just didn't seem all that bright when friends and relatives were coming home from the war in body bags.

Then came STAR TREK, showing not only that there would be a future, but that it worked. The first view of the starship Enterprise seen in that long ago television premiere in 1966 was astonishing to behold because it looked like something from out of the future! It resembled nothing like any terrestrial design currently in the works or under consideration, and that's exactly how the future would look—different than we can presently imagine.

But why did the popularity of STAR TREK endure into the '70s when everyone connected with the show considered it in the past tense after the last set was struck in 1969? There was something at its core which shone through that made the whole greater than the sum of its parts. There was a special something which struck a responsive chord in many, many people. It held something people were looking for; something which they sought for but didn't find again until STAR WARS exploded on the scene in 1977. As much as fans of either might object, the success of the two are inextricably linked.

Optimism was the keynote in STAR TREK and STAR WARS, facing the future with eyes looking to the stars, no matter the squalor that lay at our feet.

WHAT MAKES STAR TREK DIFFERENT?

Slowly we met the Enterprise crew. Captain Kirk, noble and seemingly fearless, yet tortured by every death of a crewman under his command. Acting more often than not as devil's advocate was McCoy, the ship's doctor and the Captain's close friend. These people related to each other and interacted. And there at the perimeter, cool and austere, was Spock. Spock the alien. Spock the enigma. Singled out for special treatment both because he was second in command and because of his alien heritage. An outcast compared to the others, and yet in charge, making cool decisions about emotionally charged issues. And revolving at the core of the stories was a sense of being; the pressure of a living presence. People thought and bled, they made mistakes and had personal philosophies. In "The Naked Time" their most deeply rooted doubts and feelings were forced screaming to the surface. No other science fiction television series using a continuing cast had ever tried to do this before, and even more astonishing, none have tried to do it since—unless they were done as spin-offs of STAR TREK.

When SPACE: 1999 premiered in 1975, we were all prepared for something good. It didn't have to be STAR TREK, it just had to be good. The fact that it was dreadful is why there was such a violent backlash against it, not that people expected it to be another STAR TREK. SPACE: 1999 (or SPACE: 1949 as one critic aptly named it), was so awful that we felt betrayed. There was no excuse for something to be this bad. There was no reason for the writing to be that awful and the directing so wooden. Much of the same build-up of expectations and resentful backlash was experienced with BATTLESTAR: GALACTICA. You can't promise an oasis and then reveal a desert.

With STAR TREK the characters took on lives of their own, each script adding another little bit of characterization (often clipped these days by local stations to make room for commercials selling suppositories and flowered toilet paper). We grew to understand them and recognize the human qualities they expressed and represented.

THE BEST OF THE BEST

Capt. Kirk and the others are idealizations. We know that when push comes to shove that they'll do the right thing. As much as fans like to talk about the good characters that Kirk, Spock and McCoy are, they don't really possess the normal human foibles of you and I. The worst that one of them might do is get angry and make a snide remark, which they'll meekly apologize for later, but when it comes to ethical choices, they're infallible.

A case in point is Harlan Ellison's "The City On The Edge Of Forever." In the crucial scene where Edith dies, Harlan wanted to have Kirk try to save her despite knowing what her continued life would mean. Kirk would have failed but he still would have tried to save her. This is how Harlan's version, which he won the Writer's Guild Award for, reads. Gene Roddenberry felt that Kirk wouldn't act like that. That he would do the right thing when the time came, no matter how painful. Thus Roddenberry rewrote Ellison's screenplay to have Capt. Kirk deliberately prevent McCoy from saving Edith's life. Kirk experienced great anguish, but he did the right thing. And yet in Ellison's screenplay the point was made that the same thing could have been accomplished by bringing Edith back with him to the future, rather than just letting her be run down in the street like a dog.

So although the characters in STAR TREK are enduring, and in many respects act more believably and with more depth than those on LOST IN SPACE, SPACE: 1999 and others, they are still idealizations. The TREK characters look like genuine human beings in comparison because it's the only time the attempt has been made on any level to have continuing characters in an extraterrestrial SF series act like human beings would in similar situations. They may ultimately be expected to be noble and unblemished, but they do at least agonize over the decision and the philosophical and ethical principles involved. On BATTLESTAR: GALACTICA, their idea of human characterization was to have a little boy become almost catatonic over the death of his pet, and yet accept with equanimity the death of his mother.

STAR TREK, whatever the individual reasons different people have for admiring it, was ultimately a safe port; a place of optimism which said, "There will be a future," while ignoring whether the thorny and deeply troubling social issues of today will still plague the undercurrents of that society. It served a certain purpose, one which people were seeking for themselves, and it continues serving it to this day.

THE CAPTAIN

William Shatner on March 28, 1978 at the Paramount Studios Press Conference announcing STAR TREK: THE MOTION PICTURE   © 1978 Ron Galella Ltd.

CHAPTER 1

CAPTAIN JAMES TIBERIUS KIRK

As Martha Kirk lay in her hospital bed, about to deliver her second son, her husband George arrived just in time to see their child take his first breath. George worked in Starfleet, and was gone for long periods of time. But for this occasion he'd been able to get a week-long pass to visit his family on Earth. They named the child James Tiberius Kirk.

The family lived on a small farm in Iowa, and now that George had two sons to care for, he applied for a ground posting so he could be with them and his wife. After six months, his tour on board the frigate Quicksilver was finally over. Starfleet posted him on an orbiting space dock, and George was able to see his family almost every weekend. Therefore he was no longer an absentee father but was often on hand to help raise his two boys in their home on the outskirts of Des Moines.

The older of the two boys, George Samuel Kirk, known affectionately as "Sam" by his younger brother Jimmy, took his little brother with him everywhere. They were as close as shadows, although they were as different as night and day. Sam's interests drew him to the Earth sciences: biology, botany, and geology. But young James was different. Jim's thoughts seemed to focus forever on the stars, and on the mighty ships that traveled to their far, alien lights. He would pester his father nightly for tales of space adventures. George learned early that if either of his sons were to follow in his footsteps, it would be little Jimmy whose eyes grew big as he listened to stories about Klingons, Romulans, battleships, and distant civilizations.

As the boys grew older, Jim's strengths seemed to lie in his quick wit, his athletic prowess, and his friendly, outgoing personality. All who came into contact with him were instantly compelled by his easy nature. Sam was the quiet, studious one, coming home with the best grades, the biggest science awards and, eventually, scholarships to some of the Federation's most prestigious schools.

While Jim made average grades and was marked by his teachers as an 'underachiever,' he was well-liked by all. He enjoyed being social with the girls more than he enjoyed his homework. And even if it appeared to others that he had a different girlfriend for every day of the week, no one hated him for his high energy, and his adventurous, experimental spirit.

By the time he was fourteen, Jim realized his aptitude for astrophysics and star charting could lead to high prospects for a great career in space. He studied harder, much to the chagrin of his many female friends, and was tested and quickly accepted into the Starfleet Junior Leadership Corps. In the corps, he learned honor, duty, and discipline. He mastered all his courses, and was seen by his teachers there as a natural leader—one who commands instant respect and loyalty. Even at fourteen, Jim Kirk's charisma shone.

As a fair and determined leader, Jim's popularity grew. He maintained his interest in athletics, and took top honors in track and field as well as self-defense courses. In high school, his track and field team from the JLC won first place in the general state high school competitions.

COMMAND

It was in the Junior Leadership Corps that Jim Kirk got his first real taste of space. He'd never been off Earth before, and it was a mock planetary survey which he led that gave him his first feel for space command when he was fifteen. With Jim put in command, he and his team of a dozen other teenagers got to help pilot a shuttle up to the vast, orbiting space dock where Kirk's father worked. He fell in love with the technology, the vastness, the grace of space and from that day on, vowed to work one day on the ships that were leaving on long, exploration voyages.

The stars were magnets to Jim Kirk. He became virtually obsessed with all the possibilities those distant suns could contain. Other worlds orbited those points of light, and he wanted to see them, wanted to understand the people, wanted to find out what was contained in those distant solar systems, and beyond. The pressures of school now were tough, and Kirk became a serious scholar, grim, 'a pair of legs with books,' some people observed. He worked out his stress in the gym, finished his high school studies a year early, and at the age of 17 was admitted to Starfleet Academy in San Francisco, California. His father was probably the proudest person of all, and presented his son with a statue of a starship as a gift. The exploration class starship, both statue and real, was the most beautiful work of art Jim Kirk had ever seen. He hoped one day to serve aboard one. His dreams were filled with the sleek ship's image, and the restive hurtling of warped space.

It was during his first year at the Academy that Jim Kirk learned his first hard lesson involving death. His father, who had been on a routine shuttle flight to Mars, had died when the shuttle's air supply unit malfunctioned. It was a tragic incident that sent Jim into a deep depression. Suddenly, space wasn't so beautiful and alluring anymore. It was dangerous, dark, and deadly. For awhile, he languished in his studies. Fear made him back off, and grief kept him closed up inside himself. His mother, also grief-stricken, wanted Jim home. She pushed him to quit the Academy, take over the farm, and make it into a real business. Kirk almost relented, but his brother Sam intervened.

Two years earlier, Sam had been accepted to the Vulcan Science Academy. He had begun to learn about all the things Jim had wanted for himself, and though Sam didn't have the adventurous drive of his younger sibling, he knew that Jim would stagnate, that his spirit would die if he didn't strive for the stars. On the expensive subspace comm net, the two brothers talked nightly, running up enormous bills. But it was worth it. Sam helped Jim see the truth of his destiny. They both shared their pain of their father's passing and healed. And Jim began to pursue his studies harder than ever, with glowing results.

ADVENTURE

Jim's roommate at Starfleet Academy was Gary Mitchell, a young hotshot from San Diego who had a natural knack for getting good grades while studying little.

Gary was a constant temptation to Kirk, always wanting to go out and explore the winding, San Francisco streets instead of studying. He loved women, and like Kirk in his youth, seemed to have a new one every week. Though Kirk enjoyed his friend's 'party' nature, he did not allow it to deter him from his serious work. He grew to love Gary like a brother, though, and the two spent much of their leave times together, visiting exotic Earth cities, trying every new food and drink they could find, and playing the field hard after their studies were complete.

Kirk's Academy experience might have been far less interesting if it weren't for the introduction into his life of another cadet, Finnegan. Finnegan, older than Kirk and Gary, made it his mission in life to get the better of them. It was partially jealousy that drove Finnegan to constantly play his practical jokes on the unsuspecting teenagers. And his true target always seemed to be Kirk. Finnegan was threatened by Kirk's natural ability to lead, his top grades, his advancement in space sciences that surpassed even an upperclassman's. Finnegan took Kirk on as a challenge, testing him always, teasing and embarrassing him in front of his peers. Finnegan would deliberately sabotage Kirk's life by adjusting his sonic shower to water (and making the water come out red), by injecting viruses into his computer, and by ripping up his uniforms.

The acts were often criminal, but Jim never pressed charges. He only vowed all the harder to make Finnegan pay by his own success in the fleet. And he never let it show that what Finnegan did was actually very harmful to his well-being. In private, with Gary, he always swore to get revenge, but his wish never came true. After one year, Finnegan was caught cheating on a final exam and expelled from the Academy and Starfleet forever. Vicariously, through Finnegan's own self-destructive quirks, Kirk had gotten his revenge. And he continued to make top grades in every class he took.

After Finnegan left, things went smoother. Gary excelled at his work as well, and though he never seemed to 'settle down,' he did become more serious about his studies as the years passed. It was Gary who helped keep Jim 'even;' helped him loosen up when things got stressful. The two were inseparable on campus, and many referred to them as 'the twins who were separated at birth.'

STARFLEET

At his graduation from the Academy, Jim made the top two percent of his class. His brother, Sam, traveled the long distance from Vulcan to be with him. His mother, Martha, also came, and though she was afraid she was going to lose yet another of her 'men' to space, she was very proud of his accomplishments.

Jim Kirk finished his schooling at Command School, which he breezed through like an already seasoned pro. He amazed admirals and professors alike with his creative mind and determined drive. It was there that Jim modeled himself and his career after Garth of Izar, his personal hero next to Abraham Lincoln and the mythical Captain Horatio Hornblower.

Kirk's determination had gotten him through the toughest times at Starfleet Academy, and thanks to the inadvertant help of Finnegan, he had learned to control himself in times of great stress and look at the long term. But he had also learned from this to never surrender in the face of adversity.

WINNING A NO-WIN SCENARIO

Command School also presented Jim with his most serious challenge to date: the Kobayashi Maru test. Jim took the test three times, failing each time. Because he so hated to lose, he became maudlin and depressed. Perhaps, he thought, he wasn't cut out for a command career. Perhaps he'd been deluding himself all along. A few days later, he learned that the test was a test of character only, and that it was programmed as a no-win scenario. Angry at being tricked by his superiors, yet impressed as well, he decided to turn the tables. He asked for yet one more KM test, then sneaked in at night and reprogrammed the computers so he could win. The act almost got him expelled. In the end, however, his professors were too impressed to do anything but give him a swift reprimand, followed, to Jim's surprise, by a commendation for original thinking.

It was during Command School that Jim Kirk met Janice Lester, and had a very serious, intimate affair with her. They almost married, but Janice's jealousy at his command potential broke them in a very emotional, debilitating battle. Her competitive nature and his single-minded drive made them attracted to each other, while at the same time ultimately incompatible.

THE FIRST STEP

Jim Kirk's first starship duty landed him on board the USS Farragut, where he and the ship's captain, John Garrovick, developed a kind of 'father-son' friendship that instilled in Jim pure loyalty, and a drive to be one day as good a captain as John. This new hero, now joining the ranks of Garth and Lincoln in Jim's mind,

taught him much. Then came the tragedy on Tycho IV. A newly discovered cloud creature attacked the crew, and Jim, frozen in shock to see his best loved companions injured and dying all around him, could do nothing to defend them. All he could do was pilot, by himself, the huge vessel to the nearest outpost, all the while sending his helpless mayday. Captain Garrovick died during that outing, and Kirk never forgave himself for not doing more to protect his commander. Kirk took the guilt with him into future missions, never forgetting the pricelessness of life, never forgetting that one moment's hesitation can mean the difference between success and failure, life and death.

As a result, Jim became a tough leader, though always fair, always compassionate. He never tolerated laziness, and commended cadets alertness and fortitude. When he turned in his friend, Ben Finney, for not catching a flaw in a baffle plate which could have resulted in a huge engine room explosion and the deaths of many, his friend never forgave him. But Kirk knew he had done the correct thing.

Back at the Academy, Jim Kirk performed a brief stint as a teacher before being sent back into space. He got a harsh reputation for being a task-maser, and yet his students were the best in the Academy. A favorite saying among them was, "In Kirk's class you either think or sink."

OUTBOUND

Soon after, Jim became first officer of the starship Constitution. Five years on the ship demonstrated to his superiors that he was one of a kind man, a genius commander, and bound for bigger, better things. It was at the age of 33 that Jim was promoted to the rank of Captain, and earned the historical title of "youngest captain in the 'fleet." His first command was the USS Enterprise, which would change his life forever. He brought with him his old friend Gary, a friend from his days on the Farragut named 'Bones' McCoy, and met his future life-long friend, and the 'best science officer in the 'fleet', Lt. Commander Spock. Though Gary died early on, the rest of the team became renowned in Starfleet annals as the crew who couldn't be beat.

Captain Kirk commanded the Enterprise through its first 5-year mission and then retired briefly from active duty. With the rank of admiral, he taught at Starfleet Command until the lure of space drew him back to regain control of the now completely refitted Enterprise. Reunited with his old crewmates, they took the Enterprise to new glory, as well as down into terrible defeat when Kirk had to destroy the vessel to keep it out of Klingon hands. On that same day Kirk also lost his only son, whom he'd only recently learned was his.

Almost court martialed for stealing and losing the Enterprise, only Sarek of Vulcan, as well as of Kirk's own successful mission into the past to save the Earth from a strange, powerful space probe, reinstated him with all charges dropped.

Kirk remained on the Enterprise, for as he once said, "All I need is a tall ship and a star to steer her by."

CHAPTER 2

BEHIND THE CAPTAIN: WILLIAM SHATNER

His parents didn't realize how seriously the young man was taking the experience. His father expected William to eventually take over the family business, but when he was 18, young Shatner made it clear that he intended to study acting seriously in college and wanted to make it his profession, not just an avocation.

Shatner attended McGill University where he made it his business to be as active in campus theatrical productions as possible. During his senior year he produced the school's nationally famous variety show. The fledgling actor spent his summer vacations during college acting in the Mount Royal Playhouse summer stock company.

He graduated from McGill in 1952 with a Bachelor of Arts degree. By then he had already achieved some notoriety for voice work on Canadian radio, having done numerous shows to augment his practical experience. Soon he was working with the National Repertory Theater of Ottawa where he earned a wealth of experience, but only 31 Canadian dollars a week. Shatner has uncomfortable memories of this period for in order to keep a roof over his head and clean clothes to wear, he had to economize somewhere. He recalled those dismal days during an interview in the mid-sixties, when the experience was all too recent in his mind.

"Daily, and sometimes twice a day," Shatner stated, "I shelled out 27 cents for a plate of fruit salad at Kresge's lunch counter in Ottawa. It helped make my budget work but to this day I not only can't bear the sight of the stuff, but I react somewhat violently at its very mention."

Although to some, Shatner's early days might sound romantic in light of his struggles and later success, Shatner says of them, "They were hell. I got through them because in front of me was a dream. I hoped to become as fine an actor as Laurence Olivier."

AN ACTOR'S ACTOR

Shatner too a giant step towards that goal when he received an invitation to join the then just forming Stratford, Ontario repertory company. It was there that he captured the attention of the prestigious theatre director Tyrone Guthrie, who took the young Shatner under his wing as his protégé. For three years the young actor played in Shakespeare and the works of other classic writers of the stage alongside such illustrious performers as James Mason, Anthony Quayle and Sir Alec Guinness.

One night he was pressed into the lead of "Henry V." He went on cold, without rehearsing. "It was fantastic," Shatner recalled. "After the show the audience and cast cheered." That year he won the Most Promising Actor Award.

At the age of 25, Shatner won the Tyrone Guthrie Stratford Festival Scholarship and used it to move to New York City and launch himself on the next stage of his career. In 1956 he arrived in New York in a Stratford production of "Tamburlaine" which received excellent notices but folded after only twenty performances. He used the opportunity, though, to pursue work on the New York stage and in television. In the fifties a great deal of

TV production originated in New York and Shatner took instant advantage of that, managing to land one role after another without having to spend years pounding the pavement or trying to prove himself with the sporadic roles young actors tend to find.

FILM CAREER BEGINS

As soon as "Tamburlaine" folded, Shatner was offered a seven year contract by Twentieth Century Fox which would begin at $500 a week, about ten times what he was earning in the theatre. But he took someone's advice and turned it down. "I still had the idealistic dream of being an Olivier-type star. I didn't want to be a Hollywood actor." So he returned to Toronto to star in a play he had written.

That decision saw Shatner eventually refuse starring roles in such TV series as THE DEFENDERS and DR. KILDARE, and states that he has no regrets over those decisions. "I was busy making good films. After THE BROTHERS KARAMAZOV, MGM offered me a two-picture, non-exclusive contract, which I took. After nearly a year of inactivity, it looked as though I was going to be solvent without having worked a day. Then came 'The World of Suzie

Wong.' From the moment I saw the script for the Broadway show, I wanted to do it. I had MGM rip up the contract, which left me a free, but somewhat broke, agent."

The studio was only too happy to comply with the actor's request. Shatner had a "pay or play" contract which would pay the actor $50,000 for the remaining year on his contract whether the studio had films for him to appear in or not. Since MGM was going through a slump at the time and they knew they wouldn't have any projects for him, they were only to happy to terminate the agreement.

HIGHS
AND LOWS

An early high point for William Shatner in his dramatic TV work occurred in a script by Rod Serling on PLAYHOUSE 90 for June 19, 1958. In "A Town Has Turned To Dust," Shatner co-stared with Rod Steiger in a decidedly non-heroic role which received the following review by Jack Gould in the NEW YORK TIMES for June 20, 1958: "Mr. Shatner gave one of the best performances of his career. As the town bully and ringleader of the lynching party, he was the embodiment of hate and blind physical

passion. Mr. Shatner's attention to detail in putting together the picture of an ignorant and evil social force was remarkable. . . Two of the season's superlative performances by Rod Steiger and William Shatner."

"Suzie Wong? Unfortunately the play that emerged after rehearsals soured," Shatner explained disappointedly. But he gave it his best, and more. The play Shatner had read and found so exciting had been cut and altered until by opening night in October 1958 it bore little resemblance to what he had signed on for. But the show had a million dollar advance in ticket sales before it opened in New York and so was insured a minimum three month run. During that time Shatner used every acting trick he knew to alter the pace and make the play more lively.

What had been twisted by rewriting into a turgid drama, Shatner began to play as a comedy. While initially the play had experienced entire rows of people getting up and walking out, this happened with less and less frequency until things actually turned around and the play became a hit! It ran for two years, won Drama Circle acting awards, and Shatner won the Theatre Guild Award as Best Actor of the Year. He followed that up with a one-year run in "A Shot In The Dark" paying opposite Walter Matthau.

DRAMATIC CHALLENGES

At this point, Shatner decided it was time to "grow up." As he put it, "Time enough after I received financial security to go back to the classics and be an artist. I returned to Hollywood after 'Suzie' and worked in many films and TV series, always trying to have integrity about the roles I chose. But even that went by the boards after a while. In order to survive I had to work in anything that would pay me. Once I made that decision I stuck to it. To everyone's surprise I turned down starring roles in 'Romeo and Juliet' and 'King John' at Stratford just to remain in Hollywood and keep my name in front of the hierarchy."

But even his television work of the time garnered positive notices. For his performance with Lee J. Cobb in Arthur Hailey's "No Deadly Medicine" on STUDIO ONE, both VARIETY and NEW YORK DAILY NEWS had nothing but superlatives for Shatner's acting talents as the successor to a once-great aging physician grown careless in his old age. Shatner's work on The U.S. STEEL HOUR and PLAYHOUSE 90 received equally high critical marks.

In spite of fine critical notices for his film and television work in the fifties, Shatner was passed over for the movie version of THE WORLD OF SUZIE WONG. The role Shatner had rigorously established on stage went to William Holden in 1960 for the film version.

In 1961, Shatner appeared in two important films of the time. In THE INTRUDER he plays a rabble-rouser who travels from one Southern town to another, inciting people to riot against court-ordered school integration. It's a film which is just as timely now as it was 32 years ago. It was subsequently rereleased under the titles I HATE YOUR GUTS! and SHAME.

Shatner also appeared in JUDGMENT AT NUREMBURG, the Stanley Kramer directed film which garnered a great deal of attention and comment at the time of its release. Shatner was relegated to a bit part as a liaison for one of the three judges, but he was nevertheless in the company of such stalwart screen performers as Spencer Tracy, Burt Lancaster, Richard Widmark, Marlene Dietrich, Judy Garland, Maximilian Schell, and Montgomery Clift. Not many actors can say they worked with performers of that stature, much less all in the same film!

WHERE NO MAN

In 1965, Shatner agreed to star in a TV pilot for a show called STAR TREK. "I could have done equally well financially had I decided not to do a TV series in favor of guest shots and movies. But I believed in the dramatic possibilities and potential of this show," he said in a 1966 interview. "We have the opportunity to do something truly worthwhile. Science fiction can be an art form. Ray Bradbury has proven this."

But while the series did sell and ran for three seasons from 1966-1969, it brought Shatner popularity and recognition at the cost of his marriage. Shatner was interviewed in the June 22, 1968 issue of TV GUIDE, and it's a pretty melancholy piece. The actor discusses the separation from his wife which was already in progress, and whether he sold out his dreams of becoming a movie star by pursuing the immediate financial security of TV work. With the damage to his private life, he found that his long sought-after success was "empty." When a dream dies, he says, "there's such a terrible void, such a loss. I find myself clinging to times when life was a joy, a thing to cherish. Today, I'd characterize success as security and love."

Shatner had experienced another tragedy during the making of STAR TREK when, during the filming of the first season episode "Devil In The Dark," he received a phone call informing him that his father had died. He flew back to Canada over the weekend for the funeral, and then was back on the set Monday morning, masking his pain before the cameras.

STAR TREK was canceled at the end of the third season, with the last episode filmed being "Turnabout Intruder." There had been a chance that NBC would order three more episodes, and William Shatner had been promised that he'd be able to direct one of those. But he never had the chance as the network did not make the final order.

By the time the series was dropped, Shatner's marriage had also been canceled and the divorce settlement wiped him out financially. In certain respects it was back to square one. He no longer had a financial cushion which would enable him to pick and choose roles, so he wound up doing almost anything which paid well. It was during this period that he did such films as the Spanish made WHITE COMANCHE.

CAREER SWINGS

Shatner also made some respectable guest appearances on TV series in the years right after STAR TREK was canceled, but none of it was comparable to the Golden Age of television drama of the late fifties. Films such as SOLE SURVIVOR in 1969 had Shatner playing second fiddle to former BEN CASEY star Vincent Edwards. Shatner had gone back to "slugging it out," as he put it. He made frequent guest appearances on such series as THE SIXTH SENSE and BARNABY JONES, as well as playing the villain in a television movie version of the Sherlock Holmes classic THE HOUND OF THE BASKERVILLES. Numerous game shows, state fairs and other appearances supplemented his TV work.

His nadir during this period is the film IMPULSE made in Florida in 1974. The biggest expense in this independent production was probably Shatner's salary as the script is boring and mediocre. In it he plays a character who kills his shrewish wife and then stalks a little girl whom he suspects has evidence against him. The director allowed Shatner to run wild on camera and overact shamelessly. Other actors, such as the late Harold Sakata (Oddjob in GOLDFINGER), are equally misused in this tired waste of celluloid.

Shatner's finest work during this time was in 1970 in the Hollywood Television Theatre production of THE ANDERSONVILLE TRIAL. The producer felt that he owed Shatner a kindness for something the actor had done for him once years before and he chose to repay Shatner by offering him the lead in this complex courtroom drama. Shatner played a military officer just after the close of the Civil War who was prosecuting the commandant of a prisoner of war camp in the South. Shatner's adversary is played by Richard Basehart, a fine actor whom he had worked with just the year before in the TV movie SOLE SURVIVOR.

Not since STAR TREK had Shatner so dominated the screen in a performance. His sharp questioning of Basehart and his ascerbic, bitter exchanges formed the linchpin of this drama which explores both the underlying conflicts of the Civil War as well as many of the same themes tackled in JUDGMENT AT NUREMBURG. Shot on video rather than film, its theme of the breakdown of human decency and the sacrifices made during wartime is an eternal one. It remains one of Shatner's finest performances as it is controlled when it needs to be understated, and explosive when the material demands it, without straying over into any ham-handed deliveries. It hearkens back to his earlier dramatic television work and the production as a whole captures the essence of those classic teleplays from PLAYHOUSE 90, STUDIO ONE, KRAFT THEATER and THE U.S. STEEL HOUR.

Shatner met Marcy Lafferty, who would become his second wife, during the production of THE ANDERSONVILLE TRIAL. He credits her support with helping him during the difficult days he faced during this stage of his career.

THE RETURN OF STAR TREK

In 1974 Shatner reprised his role of Captain Kirk for 18 episodes of an animated Saturday morning version of STAR TREK produced by Filmation. The other principal actors returned as well, although those episodes were produced over a two year period. STAR TREK seemed dead again in spite of Gene Roddenberry's attempts to interest Paramount in a revival. In 1977 Shatner was actually signed for a new STAR TREK television series. But this was literally canceled on the eve of production when Paramount decided they could make more money from a motion picture version, thanks to the surprise success of a movie called STAR WARS.

In 1979, on December 7th (a fateful day, some thought), STAR TREK—THE MOTION PICTURE was released. While the film garnered mixed reviews it accumulated $110 million in U.S. box office receipts alone. But due to production problems the film ran wildly over budget, topping out at more than $40 million, making it the most expensive motion picture made up to that time. No one ever dreamed that many other $40 million films would be subsequently made by other studios, much less the $60 million spent on JURASSIC PARK or the $100 million supposedly spent on TERMINATOR II.

Paramount was reluctant to launch a STAR TREK sequel and blamed some of the problems the film encountered on Gene Roddenberry, the producer and the co-author of the screenplay. STAR TREK II was not even seriously considered until Harve Bennett came to work for Paramount in 1981 and explained how he could make sequels inexpensively, and make films far better than the ponderous ST—TMP. Bennett proved to be as good as his word. In 1982 STAR TREK II—THE WRATH OF KHAN was released to enthusiastic reviews and an $80 million box office take in the United States alone. Additional STAR TREK sequels were assured. But Shatner now found himself competing directly with his co-star, Leonard Nimoy. Their contracts now gave them financial parity as Shatner had been unhappy over the huge amount of money Nimoy was paid to appear in the first STAR TREK motion picture, a dollar amount far in excess of what Shatner received for playing Kirk again. Shatner was the star and was determined to make sure that no one forgot it. It was thus with some chagrin that Shatner heard that Nimoy would be the director, his boss, on STAR TREK III—THE SEARCH FOR SPOCK.

DIRECTING

Following the release of STAR TREK III, an interview with William Shatner appeared in the July 6th, 1984 edition of the SAN DIEGO UNION. In it the actor had his own say about the film and the peculiar situation he found himself in being directed by his long-time co-star.

"The relationship between Leonard and me is hard to put into words," Shatner said. "It sounds trite, but he and I are brothers, in flesh and spirit. We're very, very close. So there was an awkward time for me, and for Leonard, too, I'm sure, on STAR TREK III. Suddenly one of two equals is the boss, and it's hard to accept. So there was a period of a couple weeks when I felt alone, deserted, abandoned.

"It was a situation that could have put a hell of a strain on our relationship, but it not only survived, it got stronger, I think. We both adapted, which wasn't as tough for me as it might have been because Leonard is an outstanding director, very sure of himself but also receptive to ideas."

William Shatner was clearly eager for the chance to direct, but he was passed over on STAR TREK IV while Nimoy repeated his stint as director. But Shatner was determined that he would not be passed over for the opportunity to direct STAR TREK V. In the SAN DIEGO UNION for January 3, 1989, an article by Luaine Lee reported in from a press event held on the set of STAR TREK V—THE FINAL FRONTIER, where everyone was celebrating the completion of the film.

"Nobody is quite sure what it is about STAR TREK that keeps it fresh and vital and worth $110 million at the box office. Shatner says, 'It's an amalgamation of all the elements like the cast, the plot, the basic idea, the action, adventure and the human drama. But you put it together and you don't get an answer. So there's something in the alchemy of what we do. The funny part is that none of us knows what it is. Like some cook who doesn't work by recipe but goes by taste and throws in a dollop of this and hopes it will come out. That's what we do when we make these films.' "

CHANCES

Shatner's continued popularity thanks to STAR TREK was evident when when he starred in the television series T.J. HOOKER in 1982. Although it was a routine police action/adventure series, it nevertheless lasted four seasons. Shatner's popularity seems to have been the primary reason for its success. It certainly wasn't because of the scripts. In the third season, James Darren was brought in as a co-star to take some of the strain off of Shatner, at his own request. But as soon as Darren joined the show, Shatner felt that the presence of the slightly younger actor was upstaging him and he worked harder than ever to dominate the storylines. The final season of HOOKER was as a late-night entry before it finally ran down. But with four years of episodes it formed a large syndication package. Shatner directed several episodes of the series and even had Leonard Nimoy appear in one episode as a guest star.

He followed up T.J. HOOKER with the less strenuous job of being host of RESCUE 911 wherein all of the stories dramatized are based on actual events. Now in its third year, Shatner credits the information the show has provided with saving hundreds of lives of viewers who found themselves in emergency situations similar to events they had witnessed on the TV series.

Shatner managed to make an even bigger name for himself outside of STAR TREK with the TECH-WAR, TECHLORD, TECHLAB and other novels in that series he has written in collaboration with author Ron Goulart. The series has been sold to Universal where it will be made into a TV series in 1994. While Shatner will not star in it, he will direct episodes.

William Shatner has continued to run hot and cold on Captain Kirk. While he stated that he was willing to gracefully exit the role with STAR TREK VI—THE UNDISCOVERED COUNTRY, a few months later he was discussing story ideas for a possible STAR TREK VII with Paramount. One idea had Kirk and Spock have a falling out and become enemies, a situation which would be resolved in the climax. Paramount passed on the proposal. Shatner may yet reprise his role of Kirk in another STAR TREK film, but it will be in the motion picture which will primarily feature the cast of THE NEXT GENERATION which is set to film in the spring of 1994 for a Christmas '94 release. This is interesting as Shatner claims never to have seen an episode of THE NEXT GENERATION and stated from the beginning that he felt that a new STAR TREK series with a new cast was not a good idea.

Recently Shatner and Nimoy have been discussing plans to appear in a play together in which they would co-star as writer Sir Arthur Conan Doyle and magician Harry Houdini. The play would deal with the pair's divergent views on the possibility of life after death. The play would be based on the 1992 novel BELIEVE which was written by William Shatner and David Bischoff.

In the meantime fans will discover Shatner's innermost feelings about what Captain Kirk has done to his life in the book STAR TREK MEMORIES, appearing in the fall of 1993. It will bear Shatner's byline and be his official account of the STAR TREK years.

CHAPTER 3

A TALK WITH THE CAPTAIN

When STAR TREK VI was about to hit theaters, William Shatner discussed his feelings about the series and what he would do now that Captain Kirk, if not the looming shadow of STAR TREK itself, was behind him.

At the time of the release of STAR TREK VI, there was some debate about whether it was truly the last feature film starring the original cast. Leonard Nimoy insisted that it was but some of the others weren't so sure. George Takei had been given his own command in STAR TREK VI and to him that meant the future was wide open. But William Shatner seemed willing to accept that this was indeed his last voyage on the starship Enterprise. Yet some months after this interview, he was pitching story ideas to Paramount. The following is what Shatner said about relinquishing the reins of command.

"On this important issue I'm forced to agree with my confederate (Leonard Nimoy) that this is definitely the last one. No question about it. The studio says it's the last one, it's written as the last one, the cast has accepted it as the last one, and it is definitely the last one."

How did Shatner view his ongoing involvement with STAR TREK ending after 25 years? "Well, it isn't like it's been in my life on a continuous basis. It comes and it goes, and I ride each wave as it comes in. I'm still able to find the set. Some of the other actors are too old to find the set," he said jokingly. "But I suppose that in their wisdom, if the studio thinks that it's time to call a halt to it and give it a finale or a finality, I'm agreeable to it, and this is the last movie."

Regarding saying good-bye to Captain Kirk, the actor stated that his feelings involved both great nostalgia and great sadness. "I feel a sense of loss. It's a wonderful character; a wonderful setting in which to place the character. I love action films with some kind of content to it so that there's human conflict told in action terms rather than sedate terms. That's just my preference in seeing motion pictures. Pictures should move and STAR TREK lends itself to that genre. Unfortunately, for one reason or another, it's been decided that this is the last film. So I leave it with great reluctance and with great sorrow."

MAKING STAR TREK VI

While Shatner was heavily involved with the script on STAR TREK V: THE FINAL FRONTIER, he admitted that he had no real input on the script for STAR TREK VI. "No, I just read what they were doing and thought it was good," he said regarding the Klingon glasnost approach. "It's a really good idea. It's a classic STAR TREK idea in that the important issue of the day becomes part of and is incorporated into the story of STAR TREK."

Shatner had this to say about making STAR TREK VI. "Some of the physical things were tough. Shooting at night is always tough, and shooting at home rather than on location is even tougher in that the house continues on a day schedule and you start work at 6 in the evening. That's always tough. The snow sequences were particularly rough, not because it was cold but because it was warm. We did it on the set and the plastic that was used was particularly odious, and

since I had to roll around in it a lot we were coughing it up for weeks afterwards."

INSIDE TREK

Since Shatner's SATURDAY NIGHT LIVE skit about STAR TREK conventions has become both famous and infamous, he was asked how he actually views the STAR TREK phenomenon and what he finds either fascinating or funny about it?

"First of all it is just entertainment. We're talking about a series on television and a few movies, so you've gotta put that in its right perspective. And the people who become fixated on it do so for whatever psychological reasons they have. Most of the people who go to those conventions and are really avid aficionados are perfectly happy, well-balanced people who just like the magic of STAR TREK, and presumably like us as members of the cast. Those very few other individuals who are precarious would be precarious in anything. They look to STAR TREK for some kind of surcease, which is fine, too, because there really haven't been any harmful people that I know of. There have been some threats and idle chit-chat, but nothing of any consequence. So from an amusing point of view you just have to keep in mind what this is all about."

Shatner had this to say about even non-fans who recognize STAR TREK as being something of a benchmark in television. "That's what I mean. It's a phenomena. It's unique in its way, and I don't want to denigrate that and certainly a show that went on for 3 years and then has produced this kind of interest and energy and work force, there's no question that it is a benchmark. I'm very proud and delighted to be part of it."

LIFE IN TREK

Shatner is very thankful for his Star Trek life. "It's been something that has given me great opportunities that I wouldn't have had otherwise. I've got a third novel coming out at Christmas. I wrote TECHWAR during STAR TREK V, and that [book] did well, on the bestseller lists. Then I wrote TECHLORDS, which is out there now, and TECHLAB. And then all of the other things that have occurred to me, many of them as a result of the celebrity engendered by STAR TREK. So I'm delighted to be part of the phenomena to have contributed what I have and overwhelmed by what it has given me."

Every up has its down and Shatner commented on the oppressive side of STAR TREK. "Everything that you hear is true. The invasion of pri-

vacy. The constant sand papering of your nerves as people joke or josh. It's difficult when you try to meld into the group in a restaurant, into traffic, into walking, sightseeing and just being a person. It's very difficult and that's the down side. But you can't ever lose sight of the fact that success in show business is so rare. Being able to make a living totally from this work is so unusual that I may, for an instant, be irritated, but it doesn't last very long."

While it may not appear from his overall career that William Shatner has been typecast, "Nobody ever approaches me and says, 'I would have hired you if you hadn't been Captain Kirk.' " He's sure that it's out there in the perceptions of some people.

BEYOND TREK

Regarding his professional and personal relationship with Leonard Nimoy, Shatner stated, "Professionally we've had a wonderful relationship with great mutual respect. I love to act with him. I can't remember any untoward incident. I have a deep, deep affection for him and he's a wonderfully intelligent, amusing guy.

"We see each other a lot, and our wives as well. Interestingly enough, I have another novel that I collaborated on with a man named Michael Tobias called BELIEVE and it's a story having to do with Harry Houdini and Sir Arthur Conan Doyle. Out of that novel, Michael Tobias and I extracted a play and I had a reading of the play, and Leonard read Sir Arthur Conan Doyle; I read Houdini. We did a little rewrite on it based on the reading and I think were basically ready for something more ambitious and it's within the realm of possibility that Leonard will be a part of it."

While the novels are the first published books Shatner has written, he explained that writing is something he's always been interested in.

"I've been writing all my life, either writing stuff by myself or working with other writers in trying to get some film off the ground. Then I had a hand in the story of STAR TREK V. It seems to be an evolution in terms of entertaining."

Shatner said, "I love to entertain people. I love to make people laugh and make them cry. The first step in that is writing the word. So when I'm not performing or doing something related, it seems to be a natural digression to start putting down some words. I'm always coming up with ideas for stories of one nature or another, so on several instances I'll sit down and flesh out the idea to a story and a story to a script."

RODDENBERRY

When asked about Gene Roddenberry, Shatner's reply was rather unusual; even inexplicable for someone who'd known Gene for more than two decades. His reply reads as though it is cold and deliberately worded because it was.

"I met Gene 25 years ago. He had made the first pilot of STAR TREK, which NBC didn't buy but they wanted to recast it and try again. I was in New York and he called me. I didn't know him but we met and talked about what we would do to make changes in the second pilot. For several months in the beginning of that first year he was involved very closely in the making of STAR TREK and he and I were very closely involved and we had a very good professional relationship.

Then he moved upstairs and there were other people slogging around in the trenches and so we didn't see as much of him. And when the series was over, I didn't see him at all. And then the first film ten years later we saw him around; he was executive producing it, but Bob Wise was the man in charge. Then he wasn't there for any of the subsequent films, so I didn't see him very much. I really had no contact with him, to speak of, for many years. I'd heard that he was ill the last few years, and occasionally I'd see him at the studio and say hello. But I had nothing but the most profound respect for him as the man who started all of this, and certainly had started STAR TREK: THE NEXT GENERATION. I'm deeply saddened by his death, but I really didn't know him at all."

Regarding why Roddenberry had come to Shatner to star in the second pilot, he said, "He had seen some of my work, as I recollect, but I don't know why he called me and said, 'please come see this,' but he did. I was quite popular at the time and I was doing a lot of live television and had made some films and was on Broadway."

AND NIMOY

Although Roddenberry never addressed it in any interviews, there had long been rumors that he resented the fact that William Shatner had essentially taken control of STAR TREK away from Roddenberry to some degree by becoming the star and dictating the direction of scripts. Original series writers, like Normal Spinrad, have spoken about Shatner's penchant for line counting on the series, wherein he would insist that Leonard Nimoy not have any more lines than he did, regardless of the demands of the story. It is for this and similar reasons that Gene Roddenberry reportedly craft-

ed THE NEXT GENERATION so that it was more of an ensemble. In this way no single performer could emerge with more status than the others.

Clearly William Shatner's remote description of his relationship with Roddenberry over the years ignores such obvious things as conventions where they appeared together, the STAR TREK animated series in 1973 as well as the STAR TREK II television series in 1977 which Roddenberry was producing and in which Shatner had been cast. The series was a month away from beginning production when Paramount canceled it in preference for doing a motion picture.

Walter Koenig's book about his experience making STAR TREK: THE MOTION PICTURE clearly shows Roddenberry involved in frequent story conferences on the set, which Shatner would have also participated in. So there are any number of things one can point to which cast dark shadings on Shatner's distant portrayal of Gene Roddenberry.

Leonard Nimoy clearly had some problems with Roddenberry as well. In spite of Nimoy's laudatory comments about Gene in the weeks following Roddenberry's death, Nimoy was solely responsible for stopping the publication of the 25th anniversary STAR TREK book which Roddenberry had written with Susan Sackett. Nimoy supposedly objected to some passages in the book and invoked his right of photo approval to refuse to allow any pictures of Spock in the book. This impasse was not only unresolved at the time of Roddenberry's death, but Nimoy never agreed to resolve it after Roddenberry's death either, which is why that $25.00 hard cover book, which had been slated for publication in September 1991, never saw print.

Also, in the '70s when Gene Roddenberry was largely making his income from giving talks and making convention appearances, Leonard Nimoy filed a grievance with the Screen Actor's Guild against Gene Roddenberry because Gene wouldn't stop showing the STAR TREK blooper reel at conventions. Nimoy had objected to it, feeling that it made him look foolish, plus he felt that outtakes were not covered by the contract he had signed at the time he did the series. [This can be verified by checking the files of the Hollywood trade papers of the time.]

So, however cold and distant Shatner's comments about Gene Roddenberry are, he at least did not present a pretense of praise and affection for a man he apparently had not gotten along with in recent years. What all of this ultimately says about William Shatner, Leonard Nimoy or Gene Roddenberry is up to the reader to decide.

FRONTIERS?

Shatner was asked the inevitable questions about STAR TREK V and how he felt about the way the film turned out. In spite of the image of failure attached to the picture, the actor/director was quite willing to discuss how it was received by the public and the fact that some perceived it as being not as successful as the previous STAR TREK motion pictures.

"It's just a general perception," Shatner remarked concerning the reputation the picture has gotten. "It did not make as much money as the others. They tell me it fell about 18% short. But apparently that summer was the first summer that these blockbuster movies were released every two weeks. BATMAN came shortly after our picture was released, so the tendency is to blame the release scene pattern rather than anything else.

"As for notices and things, people say, 'I don't share this, but I heard that it didn't get good notices,' or whatever, when in fact it did get good notices. THE LOS ANGELES TIMES, Gary Franklin [a reviewer on a TV news show], and he's a tough reviewer, and THE L.A. DAILY NEWS all lauded it. I felt that it was flawed and that I didn't managed my resources as well as I could have. I also didn't get the help in managing my resources as I could have. I thought it was an interesting story; an interesting attempt at a story. And I thought that it was a meaningful play. It carried a sense of importance about it, and technically it went well.

"We hired a lot of different people. We didn't go after the Lucasfilm people. We went to New York and got other special effects people. So we experimented and I had to learn a great deal, not only about film but about the politics of film on that picture. I don't think I'll make those same errors again." But it didn't discourage Shatner from wanting to direct another movie. "On the contrary. It made me froth with ambition."

While Shatner has expressed no interest in appearing in front of the camera on THE NEXT GENERATION, he'd be happy to direct a big screen outing of the series when it finally moves from TV to motion pictures, a fact long predicted and never disputed.

LIFE OUTSIDE TREK

A hobby that Shatner has been able to indulge because of his successful film career is the raising of American saddle bred horses. "Somebody once said don't own anything that eats while you sleep; I've got too many of those." The horses are raised on a farm in Kentucky.

Shatner is also still regularly heard and seen as the narrator of RESCUE 911, but is it really as satisfying as starring in a series? "It isn't, but it's a great show. I think it fulfills all the criteria for great television. It has provided me with the most humor. I've laughed out loud more at 911 in some of those episodes, and I have been moved to tears more often by 911. It has saved, documented, around 70 lives, but it is far in excess of that because people keep coming up to me and saying, 'My aunt's life was saved but they didn't write a letter in.' So I know that it's in the hundreds of lives that have been saved.

"Not only that, but we've brought a lot of publicity to the Emergency Medical System which has helped get quality people into dispatchers and emergency medical technicians. And doctors who are interested in emergency medicine have said that as a result of this show they have become emergency doctors. There's a great need for emergency centers. Rather than closing them we should be opening them because it is frequently the only medical attention people can get because of the cost of medicine being so high. So that from every point of view it's a great show and I'm just very proud to be connected with it."

THE SCIENCE OFFICER

Leonard Nimoy   © 1984 Ron Galella Ltd.

CHAPTER 4

MISTER SPOCK

Spock's parents, Vulcan Ambassador Sarek and his human wife, Amanda, wanted a child together, but their chemistry was incompatible for a successful, normal conception. So they turned to the Vulcan Science Academy and the Vulcan Medical Research Facility for help. Apparently, they were not the first Vulcan/human couple to attempt the creation of a child. But all other attempts had, to date failed. Even so, they agreed to try. They were told: "An Earth/Vulcan conception will abort during the end of the first month. The fetus is unable to continue life once it begins to develop its primary organs. " (Taken from an interview with Gene Roddenberry, INSIDE STAR TREK, Columbia Records, 1976.) Further records indicate, "The fetus, Spock, was removed from Amanda's body at this time, the first such experiment ever attempted.   The tiny form resided in a test tube for the following two Earth months while our physicians performed delicate chemical engineering, including over a hundred subtle changes we hoped would sustain life. At the end of this time, the fetus was returned to Amanda's womb.

"At the end of the ninth Earth month, the tiny form was again removed from Amanda—prematurely by Vulcan Standards—and spent the next four months of Vulcan-term pregnancy in a specially designed incubator. The infant Spock proved surprisingly resilient; seemed to be something about that Earth/Vulcan mixture which created in that tiny body the fierce determination to survive." (again from INSIDE STAR TREK.)

BETWEEN TWO WORLDS

For Spock, his dual nature was extremely confusing, especially when he was a young child. Sarek constantly demanded of him a proper Vulcan stature and attitude, even at the age of two, while Amanda, with her emotional spirit and outward displays of affection for her child, encouraged Spock to laugh, play, and be like human boys. Trying to please both parents only further confused the boy, and as a result, he began to feel the beginnings of what it was like to be an outsider, even in one's own home.

Sarek had wanted to send Spock away to be trained in the Vulcan Way. But Amanda would hear nothing of it. He was still just a 'baby,' and she wanted to raise him herself. As a result, Spock's earliest lessons involved more about emotions, and less about logic. This would make it hard on him as he got older,.

Sarek saw this and grew concerned. Though his son was half-human, his emotional make-up was also Vulcan. He needed discipline, he needed to learn to get along in the society in which he was born. Plus, Spock's emotional displays embarrassed him when he and Amanda would travel, or visit friends. He could already see how Spock was ostracized by other children his own age. They teased him unmercifully, called him 'alien.' Still, he allowed Amanda to remain in charge.

A sehlat, which is like a huge teddy-bear with six-inch fangs, became Spock's only true friend in those early years. I'Chaya followed his young master everywhere, became both playmate and listening post, was witness to all Spock's confusing, emotional displays. Spock rode I'Chaya around the yard, made up fantasy scenarios involving warriors and violent battles in which he and I'Chaya came out the victors and heroes. He lived in his fantasy world much of the time, and ignored the outside world that he was coming to recognize as all-too cruel to him.

Spock's peers saw him playing in his yard, and often watched at a distance as his elaborate schemes and scenarios became very real to him. One boy, Sefek, teased him constantly from the fence. He called Spock 'inferior' and 'foreign,' which made the boy all the more introverted.

Sarek decided then to take charge and begin Spock's lessons in the Vulcan Way. He tutored his son himself, showing him how to master the Vulcan nerve-pinch, teaching him how to meditate and discipline the 'self,' and reviewing again and again the history of Vulcan, most notably the accomplishments of Logic's forefather, Surak.

When Spock was six years old, he had an equal grasp of human as well as Vulcan beliefs. That his parents were so different still confused him, and because of his human make up, he still had trouble controlling his emotional side. His emotions terrified him at times, and he grew to hate his human half as friends began to call him 'half-breed.'

VULCAN WAY

When Spock turned seven, Vulcan society, as well as his father, forced him to make a decision between accepting the Vulcan Way completely into his nature, or choosing the less-respected human path. Spock revered his father, and strived always to please him. It came as no surprise to Amanda, then, when he announced he had decided to follow Vulcan custom only. Though Sarek was very proud, Amanda mourned the 'death' of her human son. Spock himself had other reasons as well. He concluded that the only way to make his peers respect him was to conform to their way of life. He desperately needed to feel accepted somewhere. Though the human path would have been the easier route, he resented humanity, also, for making the other children tease him. The Vulcan Way seemed to be his best and most logical choice.

It was difficult at first for Amanda to just 'let Spock go.' For awhile, she continued to try to 'coddle' him when he would come home from school with a stiff upper lip and she knew he'd been taunted and mentally tortured yet again by the other students. But Spock pushed her away, learning early on that to give in to the weakness of allowing his mother to 'right' the 'wrongs' only made it harder for him to go back and face his tormentors.

Just before the end of Spock's seventh year, the traditional kahs-wan approached. This was the Vulcan test of manhood, and every boy went through it. The test required the boy to spend a duration of time alone in the desert using all the survival techniques he had learned in special classes, and thus proving his worth to all of Vulcan as a person to be respected and revered. Spock looked upon the test as more than just survival and a hope for respect. He saw it as a determining factor in his success at being Vulcan. If he failed, he would be relegated to human status, no matter how 'Vulcan' he became. Therefore, he had to succeed. The stakes were his very identity.

DESERT FURY

A distant cousin of the family named Selek was of great help to Spock during this trying time. He seemed to be the only one who understood what Spock had to gain and lose in the kahs-wan. Still desperate to succeed, Spock decided to test himself before the 'official' kahs-wan. He left for the desert on foot, at night, with his loyal I'Chaya following. The cousin, Selek, also followed at a discreet distance. A le'matya seemed to come from nowhere, hungry and large and terrifying. It wanted Spock for its next meal. I'Chaya was severely injured in the defense of his master's life. Though the sehlat, along with Selek's help, had succeeded in killing the le'matya, the poison of the carnivorous desert creature had entered I'Chaya's veins through gashes and bites. I'Chaya was suffering. Selek stayed with the pet while Spock went for help. The healers could do nothing, and gave Spock a decision: Let the creature suffer and die from its illness, or put it out of its misery. Spock chose to end its misery. As a result of his own, small test, Spock was officially branded a Vulcan by parents and peers alike. Spock never saw Selek again, but never forgot him. He passed his real kahs-wan with ease.

After the kahs-wan came Spock's betrothal. It was necessary, now that he was considered a true Vulcan and man, to bond him for the future so the fever of pon farr would not destroy him. He understood this, and allowed his parents to arrange for a suitable mate. Though he didn't like the idea, he had resigned himself to it. His parents chose for him a young girl named T'Pring. T'Pring was even less interested in Spock than he was in her. They attended the official 'linking' ceremony, then ignored each other for the rest of their childhood.

THE SCIENCE OF LOGIC

Spock's interest and aptitude for all areas of science began soon after he turned eight. He studied hard, putting his intellect ahead of all other needs. Though his emotions continued to be a problem to him, he used his studies to distract and discipline himself. His mother helped as well by distancing herself from him, though she still churned with emotions concerning her small son's turbulent heritage.

Spock continued to study and attempt to master Vulcan disciplines, as well as his academic studies. He did not excel as quickly there, and it took him a lot longer than other children to fully learn the proper mental techniques for mind-melds, self-healing trances, and meditation in place of sleep. He worked hard. He never gave up.

By the time he was twelve, he had mastered the same levels as his peers, and yet they still continued, at times, to tease him, and to call him names. No one could seem to forget the emotional little boy he had been. They seemed to believe that deep inside Spock there was still that touch of alien humanity that tainted him, and made him different.

ALONE AMONG HIS PEOPLE

In his teen years, Spock spent more and more time alone. His social graces were not allowed to develop, and therefore he had a hard time interacting with others, especially those of Vulcan blood who were his own age.

Though Spock's interest in science only continued to increase, his loyalty to Vulcan was waning. His peers, both past and present, continued to reject him, and he could not help but feel a desperate need to escape the continued mental torment of being different on his own planet of birth. He knew Sarek was looking forward to him attending the Vulcan Science Academy, but the more Spock thought about that, and realized he would be working with people who still saw him as an inferior, the more he realized the need for change. He knew that among the stars, there were an infinite number of life forms, and uncounted numbers of alien civilizations. Out there, everyone was different. Perhaps those differences would serve to make him feel as if he fit in. Secretly, he applied to Starfleet Academy. He was accepted immediately.

BETWEEN FATHER & SON

When Spock finally told his father about the acceptance, and about his decision to leave and not go to the Vulcan Science Academy, Sarek reacted negatively. If a Vulcan could show anger, then Sarek did. It was the only time Spock saw that his father really did have emotions, and that even the finest of disciplines couldn't always keep them under control. Sarek wanted Spock to have no part of an organization that instigated war. He argued for hours with Spock, telling him that they would require him to kill, and that if Spock did, he would relinquish all that was Vulcan in doing so. Spock firmly defended his position, telling his father his mind was made up, that Vulcan did not hold his destiny, that he could no longer tolerate the bigotry and ostracization. Sarek refused to see any logic in Spock's arguments, and called his son overly 'sensitive' and 'confused.' He gave Spock an ultimatum that shocked the boy. If Spock left, he would disown him as his son. Sarek vowed never to speak to him as a 'father' again.

Stunned, filled with an untapped grief, Spock still knew his decision was the correct one. He packed his belongings and left his home. In ShiKahr spaceport, he booked a one way passage on a shuttle bound for Earth. He was greeted there by enthusiasm. Starfleet wanted Vulcans in their program, and gave him everything he might need: an apartment, clothing a food allowance, and the best teachers they had to offer.

THE ACADEMY

For a long time, the distress of his upset with Sarek continued to distract and depress Spock. He buried himself in his studies, but the pain lived inside him, unquenchable. His worst skills were social skills, and he remained introverted. Starfleet demanded he seek psychological counseling, which Spock did willingly, but to no avail. Spock was not to be easily brought out of his shell, and was accepted peripherally by his peers at the Academy as 'quaint' and 'aloof'. At least these terms were less hurtful, and Spock found that even though he was still an alien among humans, he was better off.

Spock excelled in all his classes. Theoretical sciences were his strongest interest. A paper he wrote on the subject, which was published in The Makropyrios Report garnered much interest. A prestigious science university offered him a scholarship for one semester, which Starfleet encouraged him to take. It was there he met Dr. Georges Mordreaux, a professor and theoretical physicist. They became

friends, Mordreaux helping the fill the void left by the abrupt sealing off of Sarek's support and love.

He returned the Starfleet Academy and graduated at the top of his class. Though he had no interest in command, he decided to round out his education and attend one year of command school. He did well in both the physical and academic requirements, though his leadership skills remained weak. Still, working with others more closely helped him 'come out of his shell'. On the Kobayashi Maru test, Spock's logical, unemotional approach intrigued his superiors. They gave him good marks, describing his solution and character traits as 'unique'.

LIFE AMONG THE STARS

Upon his graduation from Command School, Spock's first posting was the USS Lexington as an assistant science officer. Out among the stars, Spock felt for the first time 'at home.' The alien worlds and flickering lights intrigued not only his scientific mind, but his emotional thoughts as well. He thrilled to learn of new civilizations; to see and touch things no one had seen or touched before. Though he still remained aloof, most of his crewmates accepted him for the excellent scientist he was, and demanded no more from him. Often, people even forgot he was, indeed, half-human.

His work on the Lexington earned him a distinguished reputation. He became a top science officer, and won the Gold Star With Cluster when his work helped to end the plague of the Orion Beta Virus.

His cadet cruise came to an end, and with it came a promotion to full Lieutenant. He skipped one grade, that of ensign, altogether, and his worth to Starfleet became well-known. He was offered a job on the all-Vulcan ship, USS Intrepid, which was manned by 430 Vulcans. The Intrepid was to be strictly a science vessel, maintaining Vulcan's pacifism as its main priority. Spock was offered a revered position, plus another promotion, but he turned them down. He did not come to the stars only to find himself among the very people he'd tried to escape. Instead, he felt the better offer to be from a ship called USS Enterprise.

THE FUTURE

Spock's first captain aboard the Enterprise was Robert April. But soon after their initial shakedown cruise, April was promoted to commodore and left the ship. The new captain, Christopher Pike, took over, and he and Spock formed what seemed to be an instant friendship and rapport. Pike was a no-nonsense man who enjoyed Spock's

highly professional nature and continually praised him for his quick-thinking. Because Pike also had a reserved and distant personality, they understood each other well, and both men enjoyed games of strategy together, such as chess, and hand-to-hand combat.

After one year, Spock was promoted to Lt. Commander, and left the ship temporarily to do a teaching stint at the Academy, as was required by command grade personnel. He soon returned, with Pike welcoming him back enthusiastically. Pike was the first real friend Spock had ever had, and he looked up to him as a sort of hero, wanting to prove his worth to him again and again.

Two five year missions went by. Starfleet was pushing their fleet of starships further and further into the unknown, and the rewards were proving worthwhile. Spock headed the Enterprise's science department. He still continued to remain aloof, but the crew did not seem to mind. The ship's first officer, "Number One," seemed as unemotional as Spock and Pike, and thus the attitude became one of normal conditions on the bridge of the famous ship.

Spock went on to win many more awards and commendations, both for his work for Starfleet, and his extracurricular activities in scientific research. Command School training came in handy when he led science expedition teams to alien worlds for study. After the Talos IV incident, he received another special commendation. Soon after, Pike was promoted and transferred off the ship.

ENTER: KIRK

With an untried captain at the helm—the youngest in fleet history—replacing Captain Pike, Spock found himself again among strangers. The crew compliment had almost completely changed. Instead of the reserved traits of Pike and "Number One," the new crew were boisterous and outgoing. The new captain, James T. Kirk, overwhelmed Spock at first. The first officer, Gary Mitchell, was rude and abrasive, his jokes often hurtful and bigoted. But Spock soon saw the value of his new commander, as Kirk did not laugh or put up with the jokes, and seemed to share an interest in both Spock's Vulcan nature and three-dimensional chess. Their friendship formed slowly, solidly, and he did not realize that it was the prelude to a personally and professionally heroic partnership that would go down in the history of Starfleet.

Spock became a legend, both in Starfleet and on Vulcan. T'Pring grew less interested in becoming the consort of a legend and conspired to have Spock reject her on the day of their wedding. She succeeded and Spock returned to the realm he knew best—Starfleet. He remained on the Enterprise throughout the 5 year mission under James T. Kirk and then he withdrew in order to settle once and for all his inner conflict between his human and his Vulcan nature.

Returning to the Enterprise, Spock found himself able to accept the duality of his nature as a positive thing, rather than a reason for constant battle. He stayed with the Enterprise for many more years, and when he did leave Starfleet it was to follow in the footsteps of his estranged father and become an ambassador.

CHAPTER 5

BETWEEN THE EARS: LEONARD NIMOY

Leonard Nimoy was born in Boston in 1931, the son of Jewish immigrants from the U.S.S.R. He showed an early interest in the theater, making his stage debut in a production of "Hansel and Gretel" at the age of eight. Following high school, he studied briefly at Boston College, only to pack up and take the three-day train trip to California, with only six hundred dollars to his name, in pursuit of an acting career.

Nimoy was married to Sandi Zober, a young actress, in 1954. Their first 18 months of marriage were spent in Georgia while Nimoy served out his stint in the U.S. Army. Stationed at Fort McPhearson, he was in Special Services—writing, narrating and emceeing GI shows. In his spare time he worked with the Atlanta Theatre Guild where he directed and played the role of Stanley in "A Streetcar Named Desire."

When he was discharged from the Army, Nimoy returned to California and enrolled in the famed Pasadena Playhouse, supporting himself as a cab driver, soda jerk, movie usher as well as working in a pet shop. Studies at the Pasadena Playhouse did not lead to much movie work, however. "I had started out with a love of the theatre, but came to California to pursue a film career," Nimoy states. "I always felt that I would work here until I developed enough of a reputation to be useful on the road and on Broadway."

He worked with actor Jeff Corey, first as a student, then as an instructor in Corey's classes. Next, Nimoy operated his own drama studio in North Hollywood for three years and taught for a year at Synanon. By this time Nimoy's two children, Adam and Julie, had been born and he had to supplement his modest income from teaching and acting. Such jobs included driving a cab, working in a pet shop and as an usher in a movie house.

ESTABLISHING A CAREER

Leonard Nimoy made his first appearance in movies in the theatrical version of QUEEN FOR A DAY in 1951, a popular TV series in the early fifties. He appears as a supporting character in the "High Diver" segment of this anthology film. This was followed by RHUBARB in which he plays one of the team members on a baseball team which is inherited by a cat.

Regarding those days Nimoy recalled, "When I first started as an actor, my work was over-emotional. I considered acting an opportunity to express emotions, and I took advantage of every opportunity I got. It took me a long time to discover that restraint can be admirable."

Nimoy's first actual starring role came in a movie about a youth who has a deformed face and becomes a successful fighter, until he has plastic surgery. The 1952 film, KID MONK BARONI, is a boxing picture with strange morals as a priest convinces Baroni to go back into the ring after his facial surgery so that he can win money for the church! It's rarely seen today, even in this age of video revivals of obscure motion pictures.

This leading role was apparently a fluke as numerous bit parts and supporting roles in films followed thereafter. Nimoy then appeared in FRANCIS GOES TO WEST POINT and ZOMBIES OF THE STRATOSPHERE, a 12 chapter Saturday matineee serial. He has a small role as an Indian chief named Black Hawk in the Republic B-western OLD OVERLAND TRAIL. In the 1954 science fiction monster classic THEM! his role is even smaller as he has a walk-on part as a soldier delivering a message which has just come over the radio. It would be many years before Nimoy would again be offered a leading role in a motion picture.

THE CAREER TAKES OFF

In the early sixties Nimoy continued getting a variety of roles although now the bit parts on TV shows were gradually growing into meatier roles on such series as RAWHIDE, THE VIRGINIAN, OUTER LIMITS and PROFILES IN COURAGE. His television credits for the '60s cover most of the top shows on the air at the time. Because of his rugged features, he was usually cast as the heavy in his guest appearances.

Nimoy's first real sympathetic role in some years was in an episode of DR. KILDARE directed by his past mentor, Elliot Silverstein. Speaking of the actor, award-winning director Silverstein stated, "Nimoy is one of the most patient actors I've met. He's remained gentle and dignified throughout, even when he wasn't welcome as a first-line talent as he is today. He has a gentleness and sweetness of disposition that always seeps through. He's probably one of the best trained actors around, with a steadiness of purpose which results in his being able to bear the various degrees of recognition heaped on actors through their careers. He's grown as a man and therefore as an actor, rather than the reverse."

Leonard Nimoy first met Gene Roddenberry when the actor appeared in an episode of a short-lived series called THE LIEUTENANT. Nimoy was cast as a flamboyant Hollywood director. The show's producer, Gene Roddenberry, would eventually employ Nimoy again in the new series he was already developing. Roddenberry had already decided that should he ever produce a science fiction series, Nimoy would be perfect for a part in it.

MANY VENUES

Nimoy didn't realize it at the time, but his fortuitous encounter with Gene Roddenberry would mark a turning point in his profession and rescue him from the directionless state his career was in at the time. Although Nimoy was working a great deal, little of it was in shows which would be long remembered. In fact many of the TV shows Nimoy worked on in the late fifties and early sixties appear only as historical footnotes in the annals of television today. Even the recurring role Nimoy had on SEA HUNT, which starred his friend Lloyd Bridges, remains obscure and little known. But STAR TREK would insure that Nimoy would be elevated above the ranks of his fellow everyday working actors.

Nimoy was always Roddenberry's first and preferred choice for the role of Spock. The prospect of a regular series was exciting to the actor, who, despite his frequent guest appearances on television, did not have what could be called a stable income. Leonard did express some misgivings about the part due to the unusual makeup he was called upon to wear. What if the makeup made him look like a fool? Publicity stills of him in that get-up would be floating around forever. If the show was a flop, he'd become a laughing stock. In conference with his friend Vic Morrow, Nimoy even pondered the possibility of developing character makeup that would completely conceal his true face—just in case STAR TREK was a disaster. But either Leonard thought better of the idea or Gene Roddenberry talked him out of it.

STAR TREK didn't premiere to big numbers, but it was doing okay in 1966, and the fan mail was huge. Kirk and Spock were quickly replacing Napoleon and Illya (the leads of THE MAN FROM U.N.C.L.E.) as the TV fan favorites among teenagers. But this newfound fame did not guarantee automatic respect. In 1966, Leonard Nimoy and William Shatner appeared in Hollywood's annual Christmas parade. The parade announcer got Shatner's name correct, but he introduced the other STAR TREK star as "Leonard Nimsy."

For the first time in his life, Nimoy was frequently being recognized on the street, and constantly besieged for autographs. He took it all in good humor, although he soon became weary of fans asking him where he'd left his ears.

STAR LIFE

The true revelation of Nimoy's popularity, and the effect STAR TREK was having on its viewing audience, caught everyone by surprise. Especially Leonard. During the first season of STAR TREK, NBC arranged for Nimoy to be Grand Marshall of Medford, Oregon's annual Pear Blossom Festival. This was his first real promotional trip and he was completely unprepared for the chaos. Nimoy had toiled in near obscurity for years. The concept that he had become an overnight sensation hadn't yet occurred to him, what with working 12 hours a day, 5 days a week. He hadn't been getting out much.

The parade in Medford went without a hitch. When it was announced that Nimoy would sign autographs in a small park at the end of the route, a crowd followed him there. By the time Nimoy reached the park, it was filled with people, many of them young and enthusiastic fans who all wanted an autograph. The lone park employee was swamped and traffic in the area was completely fouled up, all because of the appearance of a single individual. Medford police finally had to "rescue" Nimoy from the friendly mob as they surged towards him in their unrestrained efforts to see the star of STAR TREK.

Although Nimoy was willing to make additional personal appearances for the show when called upon to do so, the near debacle in Medford had become widely known. Macy's, the famous New York department store, declined to have Nimoy appear to promote one of his record albums. They honestly admitted they couldn't handle the crowds. Nimoy himself began turning down many requests for public appearances because they asked for him to wear the ears in public. He estimated losing about fifty thousand dollars by passing up these offers. The actor felt that this would trivialize his work on the series and reduce him almost to the level of a performing clown. On television he was Spock. Everywhere else he was the actor, Leonard Nimoy.

His popularity continued to manifest itself in a bewildering variety of ways. Spock was the only STAR TREK character to merit solo reproduction as a model kit. While Kirk and Sulu did join Spock as small figures in AMT's Enterprise Bridge model, a six-inch tall Spock was featured in a larger diorama kit which had him facing off against a three headed alien serpent. In 1975, Spock and other STAR TREK characters would have the dubious honor of being reproduced as popsicle molds. His face also appeared on a variety of series-related toy packages over the years, including 'sixties-vintage phaser rifles and the ever-popular STAR TREK disc gun. "I Grok Spock" buttons, referring to Robert A. Heinlein's classic 1961 science fiction novel STRANGER IN A STRANGE LAND, began to crop up as well. Leonard's place in the public consciousness was rock solid, and the first season wasn't even over yet.

ACTOR AS PUBLIC FIGURE

TV GUIDE featured a profile of Leonard Nimoy in the March 4,1967 issue which lead off with the following observation: "It could only happen in America: where else could a son of Russian immigrants become a television star with pointed ears?"

The article then described the picture of "The Spock Cut" in Max Nimoy's Boston barber shop, which he would proudly point out as his son to all customers. Nimoy's mother, Dora, was sometimes interrupted at her department store job by people wanting to look at Spock's mother. The article continued:

"Leonard Nimoy, who gets much of his fan mail from younger viewers, says, 'The kids dig the fact that Spock is so cool.' STAR TREK's creator-producer, Gene Roddenberry, has a more profound explanation of the character's appeal: 'We're all imprisoned within ourselves. We're all aliens on this strange planet. So people find identification with Spock.' But actress Evelyn Ward, who went to drama school with Nimoy when both were new to Hollywood, attributes the attraction of Spock to the 'great animal magnetism' of Leonard Nimoy himself.

"Like most serious actors in the comic-strip world of series television, Leonard Nimoy attempts to give the character he plays more depth than a pair of pointed ears and slanted eyebrows might indicate: 'I don't want to play a creature or a computer. Spock gives me a chance to say something about the human race.' On a more practical level, he adds, 'A television series can either be a beginning or an end. I have all sorts of things I want to do. Perhaps this show will give me the wherewithal to do some of them.' But on the most practical level of all, he admits, 'I'm having a ball. It's the first steady job I've had in seventeen years.'

"Except for the Spock haircut, which he does not alter off screen, Nimoy does not look like an actor. He is a quiet, serious man with shell-rimmed glasses, which not only correct his farsightedness but also hide the half-shaved eyebrows that are extended upward during the hour and a half of make-up which produces Mr. Spock. Only his parents and a few old friends call him 'Lenny.' On the set, where nicknames are almost de rigueur, he is always addressed as Leonard, which may be a tribute to the dignity he brings to the character he plays. His makeup man, Fred Phillips, swears that he can see Nimoy's personality become that of Spock as he puts on the makeup. 'It begins to take place as the eyebrows go on— after the ears.' "

THREE YEAR VOYAGE

Nimoy made frequent forays onto the stage, even during the time STAR TREK was originally on the air. He appeared as Izquierdo in "Monserrat" and Brick in "Cat On A Hot Tin Roof." During his 1968 hiatus from STAR TREK he starred in Gore Vidal's comedy "Visit To A Small Planet" at the Pheasant Run Playhouse in Chicago. His role as an alien who visits Earth must have had particular impact at the time.

Writing in the June 1968 issue of VARIETY, Nimoy stated, "During the first season of STAR TREK a wise director gave me this advice: 'Build in all the character elements you can find right now while you still have your strength. As time goes on, the attrition will be devastating.' I took his advice and am very grateful for it. The fact is, a great deal of talent is required to work successfully in television— perhaps even more than in features. The finished TV product is nothing more than a series of educated, artistic guesses determined solely by the previous experience of the individuals involved. Time to cogitate, to digest or to live with an idea before committing it to film is strictly forbidden. The very basic form of creativity is undermined. If you'll forgive a tongue-twisting axiom, 'Thesis versus antithesis results in dramatic synthesis. Time and creative energy provide the dramatic content.' Remove the element of time and the synthesis becomes forced and arbitrary, lacking fresh insight." Nimoy went on to reveal that, "On the STAR TREK set we've actually had rewrites arrive seconds and even minutes after the scene had been shot. Time beats TV by a nose. And the viewers finish out of the money!"

Many viewers certainly felt that way in 1969 when STAR TREK was canceled and Nimoy moved over to MISSION: IMPOSSIBLE for two very successful years as a regular. Although he still had a year on his contract, Nimoy left the series early, citing exhaustion from working as a series regular for five consecutive years. Although offered more of them over the years, he would never star in another series again, other than as a host or doing voice-overs. He reserved his acting work for the stage and occasional films.

Nimoy starred in "Fiddler on the Roof" during the summer of 1971. His appearances in those roles included performances at the Town and Country Playhouse in Rochester, Ohio's Masonic Auditorium, and at the North Shore Music Theatre and Cape Cod Melody Tent, both in Massachusetts.

Nimoy had the first STAR TREK spin-off record when in 1967 LEONARD NIMOY PRESENTS MR. SPOCK'S MUSIC FROM OUTER SPACE, on the Dot label, enjoyed a sale of 130,000 copies and produced a hot single, "Visit To A Sad Planet." It was followed by four more Dot albums. The second one, THE TWO SIDES OF LEONARD NIMOY, is Spock oriented on one side of the record, while on the flip side Nimoy sings several songs. The remaining three albums strictly featured Nimoy's pop folk renditions. In the seventies he made five narrative albums for Caedmon records, including readings from H.G. Wells' WAR OF THE WORLDS and Ray Bradbury's THE MARTIAN CHRONICLES.

MIXED BLESSING

Just as William Shatner's career had its highs and lows in the seventies, Leonard Nimoy's was little better. In 1971, he had third billing under Yul Brynner and Richard Crenna in the theatrical western CATLOW. Nimoy played the villain who suffers a violent death scene in the film. But that wasn't all Nimoy suffered in the picture. Just as William Shatner has a nude scene in BIG BAD MAMA, Nimoy was somehow roped into doing one in CATLOW.

In the 1974 made for television movie THE ALPHA CAPER, Nimoy played opposite Henry Fonda in this MISSION: IMPOSSIBLE style caper movie. Unlike that earlier series which dealt with government agents, this was a gang of thieves. The gang pulls off an amazing crime with clockwork precision and accuracy, only to be undone by the unexpected and the unanticipated—they get stuck in traffic. It was an offbeat role for Nimoy, but by no means his last departure from playing leading men.

The 1975 TV movie THE MISSING ARE DEADLY was a complete misfire, with Nimoy relegated to a supporting role which gave him relatively few scenes. Better roles were just around the corner, but Nimoy had other plans as well. In 1975, at age 44, Nimoy entered college while continuing to carry out dozens of acting assignments, and won a master's degree in education from Antioch College.

In 1977, Nimoy received positive critical notices as Martin Dysart in the play "Equus" which he played on stage in New York City. His commitment to the role was such that when he was approached to play Spock in the then-planned television revival of STAR TREK, Nimoy turned the offer down (and received a lot of hate mail as a result). The series would have gone on without him, although it was decided not to recast Spock, but to write in a different Vulcan character. Roddenberry had hoped to convince Nimoy to return as Spock in future guest appearances on the show. But Nimoy's reasons for not repeating the role went deeper than having conflicting professional commitments.

In 1978 Nimoy was singled out as one of the strongest elements in the remake of INVASION OF THE BODY SNATCHERS. Nimoy played a psychiatrist who would have people confront their problems in unusual ways. His character dominated the screen in all the scenes in which he appeared, and this was just a supporting role in the film. In 1978 through 1981, Nimoy toured the country in the one-man play, "Vincent." Written and directed by Nimoy, it was based on the play "Van Gogh" by Phillip Stephens.

Nimoy gave over 150 performances of "Vincent" during this time and it was eventually videotaped and broadcast on the Arts & Entertainment cable channel.

RETURN
OF TREK

The real reason for Leonard Nimoy's reluctance to play Spock again had actually been revealed in a syndicated column by James Bacon for December 19, 1975. This information would eventually have a huge bearing on the much anticipated STAR TREK motion picture which was then nowhere near happening. Bacon's column revealed that Nimoy received nothing for his likeness when merchandising was done by Paramount of the Mr. Spock character. The column stated, "Next time he gets cast in a series that still endures after its cancellation, Leonard will insert a clause or two in his contract. Roy Rogers and Gene Autry became millionaires with toy merchandising tie-ups." And in fact, so did Nimoy. He had an on-going battle with Paramount throughout the seventies over this very issue, but it wasn't resolved until the studio decided they were hot to do a STAR TREK movie after all.

Nimoy insisted that he was due back royalties for the use of his likeness on STAR TREK merchandise for the previous thirteen years. Paramount was unwilling to pay anywhere near what Nimoy wanted to settle the grievance, and the only card he held was the open invitation for the actor to play Spock again. Nimoy declined, making clear what he wanted before he would sign on the dotted line.

In the November 1990 issue of PREMIERE magazine, in an article on producer Jeffrey Katzenberg, it states that shortly after Katzenberg took on the responsibility of STAR TREK—THE MOTION PICTURE in 1978, "The first crisis erupted when Robert Wise, who'd been brought in as director with only weeks to go before shooting started, convinced him that they couldn't go ahead without Mr. Spock. Unfortunately, Leonard Nimoy wanted nothing to do with the movie. So Katzenberg flew to New York, where Nimoy was starring on Broadway, and spent two days listening to the Vulcan's complaints." What the article doesn't detail is that Nimoy's agreeing to do the picture included a $2.5 million settlement of his past grievances. The article makes you think that Katzenberg magically talked Nimoy into doing the movie and doesn't explain that it was money, more than Katzenberg, that did the talking.

Nimoy was the last to sign on for the STAR TREK feature, and in fact the ink was still wet on his contract when he appeared with the other cast members at a press conference announcing the making of the film. But what happened behind-the-scenes didn't always match what was stated on the record. In an article published in THE SAN DIEGO UNION on December 5, 1978, in an interview with Nimoy conducted on the set of STAR TREK—THE MOTION PICTURE, the actor stated, "There wasn't a moment's reluctance on my part to playing Spock once more. I would not have wanted to see STAR TREK made without him, much less with somebody else playing the role. Directly and indirectly, Spock is the reason why I've enjoyed 10 years of enormous activity."

MORE THAN TREK

A few months earlier, Nimoy elaborated further on why he was the last to sign for STAR TREK—THE MOTION PICTURE in a piece which appeared June 17, 1978 in the OREGONIAN. "It was purely a matter of scheduling," Nimoy insisted. "I was in 'Equus' on Broadway. Paramount was going to make a movie, then they changed their minds and decided to do a new TV series. Then they went back to doing it as a movie again. I was going to do it last spring, with Phil (Kaufman) directing. Then Paramount changed their minds, then I got into 'Equus,' and then BODY SNATCHERS came up. But everything is worked out now."

In an interview conducted by Jerry Buck sent and out over the Associated Press wire service the week of January 6, 1980, Nimoy was promoting his newest project, the TV movie SEIZURE which was just days away from airing. Then he was asked the latest in a long series of inevitable questions.

"Nimoy was just back from New York and Washington, where he had attended the premiere of STAR TREK and promoted the movie on NBC's TODAY show. Asked if he had signed yet for a STAR TREK sequel, Nimoy, who starred in the television series of the same name, said, 'There is nothing definite yet, but I gather there's a lot of conversation at Paramount about what to do with STAR TREK next.'

"He said he does want to make something clear. 'Some people have a conception that I have trouble playing other characters, that I'm too identified with Spock. It's no problem. It would probably be more dramatic to say it is. When I work in the theatre, I can feel it in the first few minutes on stage. Particularly from people who have seen me in STAR TREK. They're trying to focus on Spock and what I'm going to be doing. When I played in 'Sherlock Holmes,' he was a character very close to Spock because of his logical deductions. But there was no problem.' "

SPOCK WILL NEVER DIE

Although he didn't discuss it publically, Nimoy did not have a pleasant experience making STAR TREK—THE MOTION PICTURE. He didn't enjoy working with Robert Wise, and the film was undergoing constant rewrites during production. Entire filmed scenes would sometimes be scrapped and replaced with something completely different. The film went longer than contracted for, thus allowing both Shatner and Nimoy the right to work on their own dialogue. Sometimes several different people would rewrite the same season and the director would have to make sense of it all. By the time the picture was finished, Nimoy was ready to leave STAR TREK behind.

In a PEOPLE magazine article in 1982, he was quoted as stating that when he was approached to do THE WRATH OF KHAN, he "almost threw-up" at the thought of playing Spock again. Nimoy reluctantly agreed in order to keep from derailing the picture—but only if Spock would be killed off. When Spock would die in the film changed a couple times. Originally it was to occur in the middle of the film, but Walter Koenig pointed out to the director that it should be part of the climax of the film. As it turned out, Nimoy enjoyed doing the film and working with director Nicholas Meyer so much, that he had misgivings about allowing Spock to die after all. He remarked at the time that "anything is possible" in science fiction. Nicholas Meyer didn't take that approach and believed that Spock died in the film. The ending showing Spock's coffin sitting on the surface of the new planet was shot and added by Paramount over Meyer's strident objections.

STAR TREK II was released with the resident hoopla surrounding Spock's dramatic demise, but the vague ending which showed Spock's coffin on the Genesis planet seemed to leave it open to interpretation, which Nicholas Meyer opposed, but he was out-voted. In spite of the fan uproar, there was never any real doubt that they were leaving open the possibility for Spock's return. It made people keep asking about the next sequel, and those questions were still being asked a year later when STAR TREK III—THE SEARCH FOR SPOCK, was in preproduction. Nimoy, of course, did return, and returned again in STAR TREK IV, STAR TREK V, STAR TREK VI and in the 2-part NEXT GENERATION episode "Unification."

While Nimoy's first two stints as director on a feature film were on STAR TREK III and STAR TREK IV, he managed to parlay the experience into non-STAR TREK feature work, one of which really hit the jackpot. THREE MEN AND A BABY, released in 1987, was his third outing as a feature film director and it grossed over $100 million in the United States and about the same amount overseas. Work on his fourth directing stint, THE GOOD MOTHER, held up his participation in STAR TREK V and delayed the start of that film until late 1988. But when released in late '88, THE GOOD MOTHER garnered mixed reviews and poor box-office. This must have been difficult for Nimoy at the time as the release occurred while he was filming STAR TREK V under the directorial eye of William Shatner. The same unkind fate met Nimoy's next directorial outing, FUNNY ABOUT LOVE. Nimoy had accepted the film in spite of his misgivings about the script. He believed that the problems could be solved during production, but as many other directors have discovered, that is almost never possible.

CHANGE OF LIFE

In 1986 Nimoy separated from his wife of 32 years and several months later divorce proceedings began. On a talk show in 1992, Sandi Zober was on a panel of divorced wives of celebrities and remarked that the divorce was so nasty that she and Leonard are no longer even on speaking terms, in spite of having two grown children. Leonard Nimoy has since remarried to a Hollywood studio production executive.

Nimoy's hobbies include specializing in black and white photographic studies. Some of his work has had public shows and been published in books. He has also written a handful of books including the notorious I AM NOT SPOCK as well as some poetry books, beginning with the volume WHY NOT YOU AND I? which is illustrated with his black and white photographs. Aside from acting and directing, his favorite creative outlet is photography and writing.

Like William Shatner, Nimoy turned 62 in 1993. While he is interested in continuing to direct motion pictures, his acting appearances have become few and far between. In the early '80s he had featured roles in the TV mini-series A WOMAN CALLED GOLDA and MARCO POLO but such juicy roles have been rare of late. The one exception to that is Nimoy's starring role in NEVER FORGET, a 1991 film he also produced. NEVER FORGET deals with an actual case in which a Holocaust survivor sued a neo-Nazi organization which claimed that the extermination of Jews in World War Two was a myth. It's a powerful motion picture made by Turner Network Television on a subject which Nimoy clearly believes in strongly.

Recently Nimoy and Shatner have been discussing plans to appear in a touring play together in which the pair would co-star as writer Sir Arthur Conan Doyle and magician Harry Houdini. The play would deal with the pair's divergent views on the possibility of life after death. The play would be based on the 1992 novel BELIEVE written by William Shatner and David Bischoff.

Nimoy may play Spock once more in the STAR TREK motion picture slated to feature THE NEXT GENERATION cast in 1994, but this has not yet been officially announced.

CHAPTER 6

A TALK WITH THE VULCAN

STAR TREK VI was just about to open, and Gene Roddenberry had just recently died when Leonard Nimoy discussed what he regards as his last appearance as Spock on the big screen. Nimoy began by talking about yet another STAR TREK appearance he'd recently done, his guest starring role in THE NEXT GENERATION episode "Unification".

"I was in New Haven about 3 or 4 months ago for a convention, and I think it was there that I announced for the first time that I had just agreed to appear as Spock in THE NEXT GENERATION. The place went nuts." And the reaction since he'd done the series itself? "Pretty great. It felt like it was the right time. We'd had various conversations about the possibility earlier, but this seemed like the right time. I didn't think THE NEXT GENERATION would make it as another series. I was very wrong." For that reason Nimoy refused to speculate on whether the new series would do well if it moved into the feature film marketplace.

Regarding the style and what was hoped to be accomplished with STAR TREK VI, Nimoy stated, "A lot of closure. That was the intention and my idea was to do a closure with the Klingons." But it wasn't his idea to have Michael Dorn be one of the Klingons in the movie. "No, that grew out of what we were talking about. But it was clear that there were Klingon characters on the Enterprise in THE NEXT GENERATION. And it was clear to me that what Ronald Reagan had referred to as the Evil Empire was coming apart. The Berlin Wall had come down. I have been to Russia and seen the whole Glasnost/Perestroika kind of impact, and I thought there is going to have to be a lot of dialogue! There is going to have to be a new kind of rethinking of these relationships, and a whole new military vision. A whole new vision about hardware and all of that."

THE SENSUAL VULCAN

Regarding the Kim Cattrall character and whether there was implied sexual tension between them, Nimoy stated, "Many years ago, when we were doing the series, Isaac Asimov described Spock as a security blanket with sexual overtones." And how does Nimoy describe Spock? "That's it!"

Will Nimoy miss doing STAR TREK now, or is he sick of it, or perhaps a combination of both? "I'm not sick of it. It's been very satisfying and fulfilling. If we were not doing interesting stories, it would be a bore just to put on the clothes again, put on the ears again and go to work. But as long as the mind is engaged, you can't get sick of it."

Could anyone else do Spock, he was asked? Nimoy paused, thinking, and then said, "I don't know. I really don't know. I would think that somebody would have a tough time." And the actor admitted that he does feel possessive about the character. "Yeah, I do. If somebody else set out to play Spock, I wouldn't wish him well." How does he think that someone else might play the character? "For me, there's such a mating of the actor and the character that it seems to me it would be very difficult. But then again, these things happen." And he thinks that would be true of the other characters, like Captain Kirk, Scotty, Uhura, etc. in that there's a very close identification between the characters and the actors who portray them.

ENTERPRISE TRIUMVIRATE

It has long been observed that there is a special rapport between Kirk, Spock and McCoy. According to Nimoy, this is how it developed.

"What happens in a series, at its best, and I'm describing a process in terms of what my experience with it is on STAR TREK, is that on a day to day basis, when you play scenes that are written, and maybe you interject a word or two or a look or a phrase or an idea or an eyebrow raise. The writers and the producers, if they're on their game, when they watch the film each day of yesterday's work, begin to pick up on threads of relationships. They begin to pick up on threads of chemistry that maybe they couldn't have predicted. They say, oh, I think there's fun in the tension between this guy and this lady. Or it's funny when he picks on him. Or it's funny when he says something and we cut to him for a reaction and he raises his eyebrow. And they start to write for that.

"They structure the scripts so that you can play to that. Sometimes the pendulum swings too far, and you have to go to them and say, guys, I've been raising my eyebrow at his jokes three times every episode for the past 6 weeks. Why don't you find something else or stop it for awhile, and you have to swing the pendulum back. But that's the way it works when it's working best, when the writers and the producers and the directors foresee what's going on with the chemistry that's happening on the set and see if they can kind of feed that."

But was there ever anything involving Spock which they tried and it didn't work? "Yeah. During the series, we had a failure, I think, or at least I experienced it as a failure in an episode called 'Galileo 7' which was late in the first season. The Spock character had been so successful that somebody said, let's do a show where Spock takes command of a vessel. We had this shuttlecraft mission where Spock was in charge. I had a tough time with it. A very tough time. And I really appreciated the loss of the Kirk character for me to play against. Because the Bill Shatner/Kirk performance was the energetic driving performance and Spock could kind of slipstream along and make comments and offer advice

and give another point of view. But put into the position of being the driving force central character was very tough for me. I experienced it as a failure in that episode."

WHO IS NOT SPOCK?

In spite of Nimoy's proprietary feelings about the character, having been associated with the persona of everyone's favorite Vulcan for so long has not been particularly easy all of the time.

"I have always, maybe to a fault, taken the art of acting very seriously. I taught acting for 5 years before I started to do the series. So I was always very imbued with concepts of how an actor goes about identifying with a character and vice versa. And how an audience perceives both or the character/actor and the actor/character. I was struck one day, and I wrote about this," referring to his book I AM NOT SPOCK, "in the San Francisco airport by this strange kind of phenomenon that was brought home to me in a particular incident when a lady recognized me and brought her child to me, and said, 'Look who's here? Your favorite person.' And the kid is looking at me and is dumbfounded, really bewildered. He doesn't know what his mother is talking about. His mother said, 'This is your favorite person. You watch him on television every week.' And the kid is looking at me and he still doesn't get it. She says, 'That's Mr. Spock!' And she was wrong! And the kid knew she was wrong! He wasn't going to buy it.

"Now this is really a remarkable demonstration of this question. I understood what she was saying. I understood that she was using kind of a shorthand language that we use in our culture that says, he is Kojak. He is Columbo. She is Murphy Brown. But it's a shorthand, it's not real. The longhand would be, this is an actor named Leonard Nimoy who portrays a character of Spock each week on a television series called STAR TREK. That's the longhand. She simply said, 'This is Spock.' I was writing the book at that time, and I wrote a chapter in the book called 'I Am Not Spock,' and I explained this phenomenon as best I could. That I was born in Boston, not on Vulcan. I don't have pointed ears. I don't wear that uniform.

"I am not really logical by nature," Nimoy continued, "although I have learned to function more logically as a result of being related to the character. I have a brother. Spock did not, at that time. We later created a brother for him in STAR TREK V. I was born of Russian immigrant parents, not a Vulcan father and an Earth mother. I'm laying out all these differences. And I'm trying to explain in this chapter how this interaction takes place and what the process is to assume a character and the characteristics of a character and to function as that character 5 days a week, 12 hours a day.

"So I was exploring that, and that's what I was writing about when I said that 'I Am Not Spock,' I am this other person. And then eventually that became the title of the book because it was the most provocative, controversial, intriguing, print-getting kind of title, but it created the wrong impression."

SPOCK FOREVER

But is there a sense of relief not to be playing Spock anymore, or any negative aspects to having played the character for 25 years?

"There is no question that I will go to my grave being identified most strongly with this character, and there will be some people who will write, 'He was best known for Spock,' or he was most successful playing Spock or he was so strongly identified with Spock that he could not blah, blah,

blah, blah. Or some will say in spite of the fact that he was heavily identified with Spock he managed to accomplish X, Y and Z.

That's the way it is! I've learned to come to grips with that and I understand. There have been times that I was impatient with the press on this issue because I thought, again, it's a fairly easy, quick grab handle: Leonard Nimoy, best known as. . . or Leonard Nimoy, he of the pointed ears, depending on who you're writing for on the level of sophistication of your reader. So my great pleasure was that after 15 or 20 years of that, it seemed to kind of ease off and people began to understand that there was a person at work here doing a job.

I needed a gigantic hit like THREE MEN AND A BABY to give me some sense of an identity as a person." And was it worth the wait? "Oh, yeah. I knew that even before then that it was worth it. Given the question, would I have rather done without it, the answer is no. It was a great opportunity and the simple fact is that after STAR TREK I was never out of work. Sure, it would be a great curse if you were so identified and so successful. That's the irony. If you're identified with a character, you're successful in that character. That's a success! A double-edged sword, yes, but it is a success. The alternative is. . It's like saying, would you rather not be 60 years old

today? Well what's the alternative? The alternative is dismal failure where you have no identification."

THE MANY FACETS

On the subject of the evolution of the Spock character since his first appearance in "The Menagerie," Nimoy agreed, "It's changed a lot. There was an attempt to change the character in the first STAR TREK movie. I was trying to find a way of establishing the idea that Spock was the living alter-ego for that thing out there; that V'ger thing out there. It was on a search for an identity, and that Spock could understand that because Spock recognized that he had consciously gone through that same process and empathized with this thing. So that was the beginning of that process, really.

"In STAR TREK II, we had a pretty straight-ahead Spock until he died. In STAR TREK III we had a very different drama to play. Spock was hardly there until the very end, and then it was only physical. There was really nothing operating except, 'Your name is Jim.' STAR TREK IV was kind of a redevelopment of a whole internal life. The ideas of information, philosophy, everything, of the character. At the end of STAR TREK IV, I felt that Spock had a rather different condition than he'd ever been in before. He was on his game with his father. He was able to stand toe-to-toe and say, 'I know who I am and I'm not threatened by this relationship any more. I've grown up and if you can't accept that I'm still okay about it. It's no longer my problem.'

"In the beginning of the movie his mother says to him. 'You will have feelings because I'm your mother and I'm human and you will have feelings.' And in the beginning of the movie Spock doesn't understand what she's talking about. At the end of the movie, the father says to Spock, do you have any message for your mother, and he says, 'Yes, tell her I feel fine.' So he's using his father as a message-carrier to say that I have feelings. His father doesn't quite understand what he's talking about, but Spock is okay," Nimoy explained.

EARLY DAYS

"STAR TREK V was kind of an anomaly because the script forced Spock to be forced into a kind of a throwback posture, dealing again with the pain of his miscegenation; the Vulcan father, the Earth mother and so forth. But coming out of it again okay because he said to his brother, I'm not the kid you left behind 25 years ago. I've changed. I'm different. In STAR TREK VI, I think he really is breaking new ground, saying to Valeris, 'Logic is the beginning of wisdom, not the end.' The unspoken sentence is that it's not even everything I used to think it was. So I think he's come quite a distance and it is playing these changes that has kept me interested."

Gene Roddenberry had died just a month before this interview, and in commenting on the man whom Nimoy had known for 25 years he said, "Not only did he have a great vision, but he had a great stubbornness to stick to it. A great sense of self-assured stubbornness, even when it must have been scary. When people were saying, that's no good, you can't do that, we won't do that, it won't work and so forth.

I tried to talk him out of the pointed ears one day. I really did because we were having trouble with it. Just a simple physical, technical problem. They weren't looking good. They weren't being made right. The company that was making them was incapable of making them. We had to switch companies, and then it was okay. But in the meantime the start date was approaching and they were looking ludicrous. I went to him and I said, Gene, it's not working. We've got the haircut. We've got the skin color. We've got the eyebrows. The ears are not working and I'm worried about it.

"He said, we're going to keep doing it, we're going to keep working at it and keep chipping away at it because if you don't, because if you start to give up pieces of the vision then you end up with something homogeneous and there's no point. What's the point, you know? And he was right. There really was the famous joke where he said, 'We'll do 13 shows and if you're not happy with the ears we'll get you an ear-job.' So that's the way that went. But he was stubborn about what it should be," Leonard recalled.

REMEMBERING GENE

Nimoy went on to explain, "And when the network wanted to know, 'Who's the monster this week? Who's the heavy this week?' There wasn't necessarily one, and I tried to perpetuate that vision in STAR TREK IV. There was no heavy in STAR TREK IV. Nobody got shot. At the end of STAR TREK III, I said to Harve Bennett, if we make another one, I want to make one where nobody gets killed. Where there's no black hat heavy that we can point to and say, 'If that

person dies we'll be okay.' Where circumstances come at us in such a way that we have created our own problem. That our ancestors have created the problem for us, even unknowingly, unconsciously; not intentionally. And it turned out to be the most successful of the films and very rewarding. Nobody fired a shot in anger. The only shot that was fired was a harpoon that was aimed at a whale and never got there."

Still on the subject of Roddenberry and his continuing influence on the STAR TREK features, Nimoy stated that Gene was very much involved with STAR TREK VI. "I went to him for regular meetings on the script. Every time we had a draft of the script I went to Gene for a meeting. He was very intrigued with the idea that we would be exploring the relationship with the Klingons. But he was very much involved." Regarding stories that Roddenberry had been frozen out of creative participation in the features after STAR TREK: THE MOTION PICTURE, Nimoy dismissed such rumors out of hand. "Who said that? That he was frozen out?! No. Not true, and very unfair.

"Gene was concerned, in this particular story, about the prejudice question, because sometimes when you show people exhibiting a prejudice, even though your intention is to show that they're wrong, there are going to be people who identify with them, and who say that the people who are finding them wrong are wrong. And here you've got a couple of guys saying, 'What do ya' think of the smell?' 'And only the top of the line models can even talk.' Gene was concerned about this because he said, 'I don't feel good about Enterprise crew talking that way.' And we pointed out that these are bad people who are racist and who turn out to be assassins. He was just uncomfortable to know that there were a couple of guys walking around in Federation uniforms who will talk that way about another race."

Asked if he had wanted to direct STAR TREK VI, Nimoy said no. "It was very tough for me. Directing STAR TREK IV was very, very tough for me because Spock is a two hour makeup job and if you add that to the double job of acting and directing in the film anyway, it's a killer."

Perhaps the oddest question put to Nimoy regarding the feature films was why there hasn't been more sex in STAR TREK to make up for the restrictions which were put on the TV version. "I suppose that's a phenomenon of the fact that we did come out of television and still are appealing to a very broad audience, including kids. I suppose it's a function of that fact."

NEVER FORGET THE PAST

Another project which had been very personally important to Nimoy was his Turner Network Television production of the movie NEVER FORGET. He starred as a concentration camp survivor who proved the existence of the holocaust in a modern court of law.

"I was talking to the Turner Network people this morning and I sent them a FAX of this particular piece of information. This is NEWSWEEK for November 18, which is today, in a story about David Duke. And it says here: 'Searching for a new way to help build his political base, Duke founded the National Association for the Advancement of White People. His newsletter, the NAAWP news was a vehicle for some of his most virulent rhetoric. In an essay on the evils of race mixing he asserted that children of interracial marriages encounter frequent orthidontal problems, and damage to, quote, vital organs, end quote.'

"Then it goes on to say, and this is what I was particularly affected by, 'Dukes NAAWP carry the organizational earmarks of the Liberty Lobby, a right wing hate group founded by Willis Cartow in 1955. Duke used the one hundred thousand strong mailing list from Cartow's own Spotlight Newsletter to help fundraising for his 1988 presidential campaign. During this period, Duke attended meetings at the Institute for Historical Review, a Cartow-funded operation that underwrites scholarship to disprove the Holocaust.'

"The program that I produced, that I acted in that was on the Turner Network last April, was about the Institute for Historical Review. It was about the fact that in 1978 or '79, they cynically offered a $50,000 reward to anybody who could prove that Jews were gassed by the Nazis during the Second World War. A man named Mel Mermanstein, an Auschwitz survivor here in Southern California, challenged that offer. Accepted the offer so that he could prove that his family was gassed to death by the Nazis. And because they reneged on their deal with him, he and his lawyer claimed that a contract had been formed and he brought them to court on breach of contract. They beat them in court and they got a Los Angeles judge in Los Angeles Superior Court in 1981, who gave what he called 'judicial notice' of the fact, so that it becomes a legal fact in American jurisprudence for the first time. It is a fact, he said, that Jews were gassed by the Nazis in 1944 at Auschwitz," Nimoy stated.

MEANING

"That organization that we depicted, that made this challenge, is the Institute for Historical Review which David Duke attended during his 1988 Presidential campaign. So I think that it's an extremely current story. I was talking to Turner this morning about the possibility of rerunning the show in light of what's happening with David Duke. But even if Duke loses, it's not going to go away. I think he'll run for President next and he'll get a lot of votes! He expresses stuff that a lot of people want to hear expressed in a way that makes them comfortable to have it expressed, and particularly in the economic times that we're in.

It's the opportunity that Hitler found in Germany in the '30s. There was a lot of people out of work, a lot of people disaffected, a lot of people angry with the government. And along comes a guy that says put on a brown shirt and I'll tell you what to say and show you how we do this and they're ready. A very dangerous time.

"These are the reasons I went into this business, to do social drama," Nimoy explained, referring to both NEVER FORGET and A WOMAN CALLED GOLDA. "Not that I'm a message carrier. I'm just as much interested in entertaining as anybody else. But

I'm interested in entertaining with ideas." This can certainly be applied to STAR TREK IV, a film about preserving whales which was perhaps seen by more people than have seen all of the Jacques Cousteau films ever made.

"We looked at a lot of Cousteau footage when we started to put the film together. The question was how to get the whale footage that we needed. Cousteau's material was almost entirely in 16mm and unusable for us, but it was very educational. So we had to create most of our own footage, and if anything, our guys did it so successfully that people were so totally fooled, thinking that this was real whale footage, that they didn't win the Academy Award because of that. I sincerely believe that. The award that year for special effects went to the people who made the creature for LITTLE SHOP OF HORRORS, which was so obviously a theatrical device and much more sexy and glitzy than our very real looking whale, which was an amazing accomplishment."

ON STAGE

While STAR TREK IV was very much a crossover film which appealed more broadly to mass audiences, STAR TREK VI was viewed more as an outright gift to STAR TREK fans.

"I think you're probably right," Nimoy agreed. "We may have, in a strange kind of way, an appeal for a foreign audience that we never had before because of the issues. But I do think you're right. It's not quite as embraceable by a non-Trek audience as certainly (STAR TREK) IV was."

Nimoy was asked how his professional and personal relationship with William Shatner has developed over the years.

"We get along great. I feel great affection for him and I think he feels the same. We're working now on an idea to do a play together. I can't tell you who the characters are. I don't want to steal his thunder. It's his project and I don't want to be the one who blows his cover.

Continuing to discuss William Shatner, Nimoy stated, "We have a very, very close sense of loyalty and sympathy for each other. I greatly admire his enormous passion about everything that he goes into. He went into saddle bred quarter horses with such an enormous passion that I think he's had to devote his constant waking hours to making enough money to pay for his hobby. But he just does it and I say, so what? Are you going to say he's wrong? He's living his life every day with his great passion, and his wife is involved with him in it. He's a great guy."

THE FINAL FRONTIER

Asked what he thought of Shatner's work on the controversial STAR TREK V, Nimoy stated, "He worked very hard and he directed it as well and as capably as I think any of our other films. He was not riding on a good script, and if you're not riding on a good script, then you as a director are the person that people point fingers at, and he was responsible. He was involved with the development of the script; it was his story. But he was not riding on a good script. I've had that experience. I just finished a movie last year for Paramount that didn't work at all. I wasn't successful with the script," Nimoy said, referring to the picture FUNNY ABOUT LOVE.

Since so much time elapses between films, and since Nimoy had the advantage of not being the director of STAR TREK V, couldn't he have seen going in from the benefit of his distance that it wasn't a good script up front?

"I complained," he admitted. "I said, I think you have some problems here, and the message I got back was, 'We know what we've got, and we know what we want to do,' and having sent in my notes about my concerns, once they got them, it's not my place to say 'You must do the following. . . '

And once the tank starts rolling it's tough to stop it. You cannot draw a rule and say, 'It must be done this way.' From the day Jeff Katzenberg called me to his office and said, 'Make STAR TREK IV,' which was before STAR TREK III even opened, it was two and a half years to the opening of STAR TREK IV, for various reasons.

"This picture," he said, referring to STAR TREK VI, "I met with Frank Mancuso, I believe it was May of last year [1990], and it's hardly a year and a half, and I think we're okay. I think the picture's okay. And Bill, I think, had two years on STAR TREK V. So it's hard to tell. Sometimes the chemistry just comes together and sometimes they don't even though you've got very well paid, very professional people doing the job. Sometimes it works and sometimes it doesn't and that's why pictures sometimes succeed and sometimes fail."

The question often asked was, is STAR TREK VI the last movie for the original cast? And Nimoy consistently maintained that it was. "I don't know what anyone else is saying, but for me it's sayonara."

THE DOCTOR

DeForest Kelley at the 25th Anniversary Star Trek
Celebration at Paramount Studios.

© 1978 Ron Galella Ltd.

CHAPTER 7

DOCTOR LEONARD McCOY

Leonard McCoy was born 400 years after the American Civil War in the southeastern region of the Pan-Terra Union. This region of Old Earth corresponded to the Deep South of the United States of America and in the 23rd century it still retained the culture and pride that defiantly held to the beliefs and practices of his ancestors.

Even as a child, Leonard was a calm and relaxed sort of fellow. Like others he knew, the youthful McCoy enjoyed evening strolls among the magnolia trees, particularly in the spring when they were in bloom. In all the universe, only Earth has magnolia trees.

But Leonard's outward calm and appreciation of native flora belied a fiery temper which was aroused when his sense of what was right was offended. Leonard was born to Caroline and Harrison McCoy. Harrison—Harry to his friends—was a Starfleet engineer aboard the recently commissioned starship U.S.S. Yorktown. Carolyn met Harry through her future father-in-law, T.J. McCoy, whom she worked for as a medical assistant. When Harrison was reported lost in space with the Yorktown, Carolyn returned to work for T.J. to console herself with a career.

T.J. was a physician who refused to rely solely on gadgets but instead depended on stubbornness and faith in the healing powers of the human body. He would have described himself as just an old country doctor, an influence that only grew in his grandson. Young Leonard constantly hung out at his grandfather's office, searching through books for remedies which could not be found in the medical diagnostics computer.

TRAGEDY

A hovercraft accident claimed the life of Leonard's mother, Caroline, when she was visiting her parents on Deneb IV. The death hit both Len and T.J. hard. Len in particular hated how death could claim someone so suddenly and it strengthened his resolve to do all he could to find ways to battle unnecessary deaths that claimed people long before their time was due.

In spite of his close relationship with T.J., Len nevertheless felt very alone in the world. T.J. tried to take his grandson's mind off his troubles by taking him on camping trips in the lush Georgia wilderness. Len enjoyed these trips as he was truly able to get away from it all.

When he was in high school, Len met and fell in love with Nancy. Since Leonard was a bit on the withdrawn side, meeting girls didn't come easy for him. But Nancy saw something special in the shy boy that attracted her and she went out of her way to befriend him. She soon gave him the nickname "plum," and Leonard quickly fell under her spell.

But what he regarded as love was, to Nancy, just a special friendship. When she met an older doctor named Crater, she was quickly swept off her feet and Len was left standing in her dust. She tried to remain friends with Len, but he was heartbroken when she stated that she'd fallen in love with Crater and was going to marry him. More than that, she'd soon be leaving Earth to follow her new husband into space where he planned to continue his vital research on a distant world.

ANOTHER LOSS

Once again Len had lost a woman dear to him. First his mother had died, and now his first true love had thrown him over for a famous scientist. Len swallowed his pride and turned his attention to getting into medical school as soon after high school graduation as possible. When he finished in the top quarter of his graduating class, he found that T.J. had anticipated the boy and had already recommended Leonard for admission to T.J.'s old alma mater, the Emory University Medical Training Center.

But Leonard's victory was short lived and once again tinged with sorrow. Just weeks before his high school graduation, T.J. suffered a massive heart attack. This was soon complicated by a stroke and in spite of his damaged heart having been replaced with a state-of-the-art artificial pump, Len's grandfather died without ever regaining consciousness.

Death was battling him and winning. Len chose to drown his sorrows in alcohol. He started off toasting his grandfather's memory with a stiff shot of Jack Daniels and soon polished off the whole bottle. Now he was truly alone as T.J. had been his best and truest friend, as well as all that remained of his family. Leonard McCoy vowed that his grandfather's memory would stay alive through him as he became the best country doctor the galaxy had ever seen.

Although a brilliant student, he was also a friendless one, except for his ever-present companion, Jack Daniels. He studied with a drink close at hand until the alcohol would cause him to dose off. His only joy in life was medicine, and what he could learn from the brilliant men he studied under. Studying came easy as he'd read his grandfather's medical journals for years. Classroom study was just a review of what he'd already learned from those wonderful books. But working with patients—that was where the real adventure was. There he could duel with death and nothing gave him greater joy than to see someone recover fully so that they could be reunited with their family and loved ones. Those were the people who truly had something to live for. With his hands and his intellect Leonard learned to heal both physical and emotional wounds. Would that he could heal his own as well, he thought.

LEARNING TO FACE DEATH

Leonard McCoy believed that the human body had its own innate abilities to heal, if only they could properly be tapped and nurtured by a responsible physician. He believed that the mind and the body formed a unique partnership in self-preservation and that if a patient was properly prepared mentally, then he could battle more successfully what ailed them physically. While he recognized the importance of modern medical advances, he didn't believe in using them unnecessarily as shortcuts to a more comprehensive form of treatment. The ways of T.J., "the old country doctor," were alive and well in his brilliant grandson.

He continued to drink, though, as a way of fighting the loneliness that haunted him. His battle with death continued as well. McCoy denied that he hated death because he recognized it as an inevitable part of life. What he hated was seeing people die unnecessarily, long before their time in this veil of tears should have drawn to a close. That's what he had devoted his life to, making sure that people didn't die before their proper time. He didn't believe that it was the will of God, or whoever was in charge, to be struck down needlessly and pointlessly in the prime of their existence. If he truly had what could be called a philosophy, that was it.

THE FUTURE MRS. McCOY

Toward the end of his medical training, Len was offered a residency by the Atlanta General Hospital. He also encountered another turning point in his life when he met a woman named Honey Longfield. Len met Honey Longfield when he went to Atlanta General Hospital to meet with a doctor for his job interview. Honey was a patient waiting to see the same doctor. While they both waited in the outer office, Len and Honey began talking about life, the universe and everything and found themselves getting on quite well with one another. McCoy's down-home Southern charm about his philosophy of saving lives broke the ice between them well. Len's basic romantic nature also appealed to her.

It wasn't long before Len and Honey were seeing a lot of each other. Their relationship moved fast and grew intense. After 3 months, he proposed. Two months later the wedding was held. Len may have moved too fast because he remembered how Nancy had escaped him. He somehow felt that if he had been more aggressive then she wouldn't have run off with Prof. Crater. He didn't want to make that same mistake again. So instead he made new mistakes. Leonard got the job at the hospital and he bought a home in Atlanta so he could be close to his work.

But a young doctor in his first residency didn't command a lot of income and this soon began to show the strains in his marriage. Honey had expected to live a life of Southern gentility with a wealthy doctor, but things weren't quite working out that way. With the birth of their daughter, Joanna, the financial strains grew even greater. Honey wanted Len to set up a private practice right away, but working in a hospital where the most serious cases presented themselves was where Leonard thought he could truly make a difference. This was a philosophy Honey couldn't quite understand.

CONFLICTS

Something else Honey couldn't understand were the painfully long shifts Leonard was required to put in. Fourteen hour days sometimes gave way to 24 hour days, and she felt that he was neglecting his family. This was not the kind of loving home life Len had anticipated. He found himself being treated like a stranger in his own home to the point that he began staying away even more than was necessary as he renewed his old friendship with Jack Daniels.

McCoy had studied to be a doctor and that's what he was. The patients were his first priority. They were the ones who needed immediate attention. They were the ones fighting to hold on to precious life. Honey was just fighting boredom and what she perceived to be a restrictive lifestyle. But on the other hand Len's family was important to him as well, especially his little girl, Joanna. She needed him. When he was with his daughter he didn't feel alone, no matter how unpleasant Honey tried to make it for him. She kept pushing him to start a private practice—for their daughter's sake if for no one else's. That was a cutting blow that went right to the heart of what he'd grown up believing. He knew that he'd have to make a bitter choice, and that it would be sooner rather than later.

One summer night Honey made the choice for him, or perhaps she felt that he had already made his choice and hadn't bothered verbalizing it. Len came home from a long shift to find his wife and daughter gone. They had cleared out, leaving no forwarding address. For weeks he tried to track them down, but without any success. Honey finally let him know she was alive by having Len served with a divorce and custody notice. Len tried to fight the custody decision but when the issue of his drinking was raised he found himself defenseless.

His family gone, Leonard had no reason to try to get home sooner, and so he worked even longer shifts. He would have remained in this continuous loop of existence had funding cuts not slashed his residency salary from the hospital budget. The United Federation of Planets was reallocating money toward Starfleet in order to combat Klingon expansion near the Federation border. Starfleet had ended one phase of his career and was soon to begin another one.

BACK FROM THE PAST

A Starfleet recruiting ad seemed to beckon to him. Since his home life was non-existent and his career was suddenly in limbo, the promises of space duty seemed like a logical alternative. Doctors were always in high demand in Starfleet, and so McCoy was allowed a brief orientation rather than an extended stay in Starfleet Academy. Immediately commissioned as a lieutenant, McCoy was assigned to a Starbase near the Klingon frontier. Along a disputed strategic zone, Starfleet was battling Klingon privateers who were masquerading as pirates.

Casualties in the conflict were high and Dr. McCoy encountered more varieties of pain and suffering in a week than he had back on Earth in a year. If he'd believed that his old adversary Death stalked Atlanta indescriminently, he was in for a rude awakening when he saw the kinds of misery being dealt out in the unforgiving depths of space.

This was a war zone where casualties were unnecessary but delivered with great purpose and precision. Leonard fought the kind of needless death he hated with a passion. This was an age where combat had evolved beyond winning with body counts, but body counts were piled up nonetheless. Combat weary scouts, destroyers, and frigates came to the Starbase for repair and medical treatment for their crews. Len saw injured and tired officers all day and all night. Many died.

It was three in the morning planetside and Len was tired and aching when the emergency technicians carried in an officer with burns and contusions. The man was conscious and as per procedure filled out his own treatment sheet. As Len looked it over he was shocked to find that this man was his father, Harry McCoy.

Harry's story was a strange one as Leonard came to know how his long-lost father, presumed dead since Len was just a youth, had come to resurface in just this manner, and just at this time and place. Life is filled with more coincidence than would ever be tolerated in a work of fiction, and Len was coming to see the inescapable truth in that axiom. .

When the USS Yorktown had been rescued years before, Harry McCoy was not aboard. The Yorktown had been hunting Orion pirates and Harry had been one of a group of officers the Orions captured after they boarded the starship. Harry had finally been freed in a prisoner swap between the Orion government and the United Federation of Planets. Harry had attempted to track down his family on Earth, but the deaths of Caroline and T.J. had effectively eliminated that path. So Harry had returned to space duty, believing that he would never see his son again. Len regarded his happenstance reunion with his long-lost father nothing short of a miracle, and he intended to recapture what they'd lost over all those years.

MAKING UP FOR LOST TIME

Harry and Len caught up on their missing years as the elder McCoy recovered at the Starbase. They went drinking together (out of joy now rather than despondency) and found that they shared a mutual interest in 3-Dimensional chess. Once Harry had recovered, he returned to duty on a short-range scout ship. Occasionally his duties brought him back to the Starbase where Len made certain he spent as much time as possible with his father. After all, he had a family again.

Then one fateful day Harry's scout ship just made it back to the Starbase, heavily damaged and its communications equipment burned out. They had been ambushed by Orion pirates but had managed to escape, following a pitched battle. The phaser couplings had exploded while Harry McCoy was watching over them, dousing him in a deadly radiation bath. As a result Harry contracted a crippling ailment and was remanded to Starbase where he was not expected to recover.

Dr. McCoy used all his skill and knowledge to save the father who had been lost to him for too many years. Len was there for Harry emotionally, but his medical attempts to discover a cure were unsuccessful. The contrast between his outward show of happiness and his inward frustration and self-doubt was killing Len as fast as the radiation was killing his father. Finally Harry slipped into a coma, the notorious final stage of the disease. Len had the comatose form placed in stasis, but months went by with no hope of recovery or cure in sight. Finally Len spent a long, bitter a night drinking memorials to his father, remembering the man who had returned to life for him only to now be lost again as Death poised to claim him forever. How many years would he let his father's body reside in stasis? What must that vibrant mind be experiencing inside that debilitating shell? It was time for his father to meet death with dignity, rather than inch by painful inch.

The following morning, Dr. McCoy ordered the medical technologists to disconnect the stasis field. Leonard stood watching as Harry McCoy slipped peacefully into death. There would be no mysterious disappearance this time, and no miraculous return. It was time to grieve for his father for the second time in his life.

TWIST OF FATE

But Death was to have a bitter laugh at the expense of its implacable adversary. It was just a few months later that Leonard McCoy received a new medical journal transfer on his Starfleet computer link. There, highlighted with a special entry notation, was the announcement that a successful antidote for the affliction which had consumed Harry McCoy had been developed on Altair VI. It was a revelation which would haunt Leonard McCoy for many years, and consume him with a secret, painful guilt.

His father should have lived; lived to return to duty and battle the Orion pirates, if only for one final time. He kept expecting to see Harry emerge from one of the Starbase shuttles, just as he should have done had Leonard been true to his principles and his oath. Leonard wanted to get away from the Starbase where he had both found and lost his father.

With the Klingons living under a forced peace, Dr. McCoy was able to transfer to the U.S.S. Enterprise. With the transfer came a promotion to lieu-

tenant commander and Chief Medical Officer. He accepted them, but the accomplishment seemed hollow somehow. Dr. Paul Piper, the current Chief Medical Officer aboard the Enterprise was being transferred because he and the ship's new captain, James Kirk, were experiencing professional disagreements. Piper called Kirk "too unorthodox," but Dr. McCoy thought that a dose of good ol' fashioned unorthodoxy was just what the doctor ordered. His life began anew aboard the starship Enterprise.

There he found a new family in the Captain named Kirk and in the cool, alien science officer named Spock. They were as different as could be, but they came to be the closest friends he had ever known. He even found a person who he believed was Nancy Crater, but it just turned out to be the creature which had slain Nancy and assumed her form. So once again tragedy would rob him of someone he loved.

Through the years McCoy found his purpose again, and one day, thanks to Spock's half-brother, Leonard McCoy released his private pain so that it never haunted him again. McCoy even lived to see the next generation of Enterprises cruise the span between the stars, but for him there would always be only one Enterprise—the vessel on which he found his future.

CHAPTER 8

JUST A COUNTRY DOCTOR: DEFOREST KELLEY

Born in Atlanta, Georgia in 1920, DeForest graduated from high school at the age of 16. Not one to let the grass grow under his feet, Kelley was just 17 when he made his first trip to California, visiting an uncle in Long Beach. He went for two weeks but he liked it so much he stayed for a year. Upon returning home, Kelley told his mother, "I have a terrible shock for you. I am going to go and live in California."

Kelley's decision did not sit well with his family. DeForest's interest in entertainment was foreign to the understanding of his father, a Baptist minister. His mother encouraged rather than discouraged his artistic talents, though, as she recognized the limitations for the son of a Baptist minister in Atlanta. Earlier she has even cleared the way for him to sing in the church choir. While still in high school, Kelley did solo work and eventually sang on a program on radio station WSB. For this he won an engagement at the Atlanta Paramount Theatre singing with Lew Forbes and his orchestra.

When he relocated to Long Beach in the '30s, this changed his entire future. Joining the Long Beach Theatre Group, he formed a radio company with his friend Barney Girard. Barney wrote the plays and the rest of the group performed them at the local radio station. Off the air, Kelley was earning his living as an elevator operator.

When World War Two called, Kelley answered. But then the young actor was spotted in a Navy training film by a Paramount scout. The result was a screen test and a contract. Following the end of the way, Kelley remained with Paramount for two and one-half years before moving on.

LONG ROAD TO THE STARS

Kelley went east to New York in 1948, gaining more experience on stage and in television. But upon returning to California he discovered that Hollywood has a short memory. Many of the people he had known in New York were now working on the West Coast, such as his friend Barney Girard, who was writing for the YOU ARE THERE TV series. They helped De Forest re-establish himself in the film capital.

This led to many roles in television and motion pictures. His motion picture credits include FEAR IN THE NIGHT (in which he had a leading role), CANON CITY, GUNFIGHT AT COMANCHE CREEK, ILLEGAL, MARRIAGE ON THE ROCKS, THE MEN, VARIETY GIRL, VIEW FROM POMPEY'S HEAD, WACO, DUKE OF CHICAGO, HOUSE OF BAMBOO, TENSION AT TABLE ROCK, GUNFIGHT AT THE O.K. CORRAL, RAINTREE COUNTY, THE LAW AND JAKE WADE, BLACK SPURS, TOWN TAMER, WARLOCK, GUNFIGHT, JOHNNY RENO, APACHE UPRISING, and WHERE LOVE HAS GONE.

His various TV appearances in the '50s and '60s include roles on SCHLITZ THEATRE, PLAYHOUSE 90, GUNSMOKE, YOU ARE THERE, NAVY LOG, SCIENCE FICTION THEATRE, ZANE GREY THEATRE, RAWHIDE and BONANZA. Although he worked a lot, Kelley was verging on becoming typecast.

"For ten years I played western heavies mainly," said Kelley. "Then Gene Roddenberry considered me for a part and asked if I had any objections to doing my hair differently. I had been wearing it long, for westerns." Roddenberry wanted a brainy, Kennedy look and asked Kelley to go to Jay Sebring, a famous men's hair stylist in Hollywood. "It was expensive," said Kelley. "It cost me thirty-five dollars, but I had confidence in Roddenberry."

Roddenberry had wanted to use Kelley in the first STAR TREK pilot, "The Cage," but Paramount rejected the idea as they saw Kelley as an actor who played villains, not sympathetic doctors. But Roddenberry persisted, having Kelley star in two TV pilots for him, one about a San Francisco attorney and the other as a policeman. Finally Paramount reversed their decision, but not until after the second STAR TREK pilot had been filmed. Kelley joined the cast once the show was picked up as a series.

BREAKING THE STEREOTYPE

"I'd never been in a series before," Kelley explained. "I made a drastic change with this role. Roddenberry went out on a limb for me. The town had forgotten the actor I used to be. Then Roddenberry pulled me out of a big rut. I feel very lucky."

Not lucky enough that he wasn't willing to complain in print about his perceived grievances.

TV GUIDE featured DeForest Kelley in the August 24, 1968 issue. The article opened by discussing how he began as an actor at Paramount back in 1946, and shortly thereafter a fortune-teller told him that his greatest success would not come until after he was 40, a suggestion the young Kelley dismissed. But in fact that is what happened. While working regularly over the years, Kelley still failed to achieve much in the way of recognition until he was in his 40's and was signed as the co-star of STAR TREK. But even in 1968, with the series renewed for its third season, Kelley wasn't entirely happy with his status on the show, as he told TV GUIDE that year:

" 'When I see the trade papers, after a whole season, still list only Bill Shatner and Leonard Nimoy as co-stars, I burn a little inside,' says De (pronounced Dee) Kelley. 'I've had a rough road in this business, and billing can be an actor's life's blood. What I want, as a co-star, is simply to be counted in fully. I've had to fight for everything I've gotten at STAR TREK, from a parking space at the studio to an unshared dressing room, and sometimes the patience wears raw. I know that my role is more passive. I know that Bill and Leonard have the easier parts to write for. But I've been through episodes where I'm standing there, without a word, for 12 pages of dialog. Once I got left out of an episode entirely. I went to the writer—he also has producer status on the show —and he said, very apologetically, 'De, I'm sorry, but it was an oversight.' An oversight! If a producer-writer on my own show forgets me, then I've got problems!'

Later in the same article, Kelley related a touching personal story about his father.

"Shortly before his father died, in 1966, Kelley unburdened his thoughts in a long letter. He says: 'I told my father that as I look back, remembering how he captivated all of us with his sermons, he was probably the real reason I became an actor. I didn't realize it, but I wanted to be an actor like him. A good preacher, like a lawyer, is a good actor—and my father was a good preacher.'

"In some ways De Kelley remains Southern to the core. On New Year's Day he cooks black-eyed peas with red-eyed gravy—for luck in the ensuing year. And he still cherishes small triumphs. When his name ran for the first time this year in a TV GUIDE crossword puzzle, his wife clipped the page and framed it to hang on the wall. 'It's not an Oscar or an Emmy,' says De Kelley, 'but to an actor it's something.' "

SPOCK AND McCOY

Regarding the famous tension between Spock and McCoy, DeForest Kelley tried to use elements of comedy and drama in the relationship. In a 1974 interview, Kelley stated, "I just gently tried to mix it with McCoy because of the unique situation that was involved between Spock and McCoy. I never wanted it thought for a minute that McCoy truly disliked him, because he didn't. McCoy had great respect for Spock and I thought and felt that the

best way, was to somehow lighten it with an expression or a line. I did that very purposefully. I didn't want to lose fans by being too hard with Spock under certain circumstances. McCoy liked him. It became a kind of battle of wits.

"Leonard [Nimoy] and I both worked on these things, you know. We discussed them at great length, as to how they should be played. We all felt very deeply about the show and worked very hard on it. The show is unique inasmuch as that between scenes we never sat down and read a book. Usually on a motion picture set you'll see an actor reading the trade papers or something between scenes. Not on STAR TREK. The whole cast always went to the rehearsal table with the director and we began to break down future scenes that we were going to do and work at a table between scenes, very much like they used to do between scenes of live television in New York. This had a great bearing on the show. No one was out just running around or loafing or sleeping in a dressing room. They were preparing for the next scene.

"We generally shot seven days, depending on the script. We even went eight days on them. We worked long hours, and there were many nights until eight-thirty or nine. Leonard and I both had early make-up calls. We had a very large cast, so our make-up calls were around six or six-thirty in the morning. On many nights we would not get home until ten. You just have something very light to eat and go to bed, and you're up again the next morning at five.

"That was our first year. The second year they began to be a little more organized and they were able to schedule things so it really wasn't so rough on us. The first year was pure hell, but I think we did our best work in the first year when I look back."

HIGHS AND LOWS

One of DeForest Kelley's favorite episodes was the one where he wore the most make-up on the original series. That was in the episode "The Deadly Years." "I enjoyed doing that because it gave me an opportunity to do something that I would never be called upon to do." As his character aged, Kelley had him become more and more the old-fashioned country doctor that McCoy really envisioned himself as. "Yes, I began to fall back. I had that in mind from the beginning, that the older he became, the more he would fall back into what he really had a

feeling in his heart for. Fortunately, it worked very well. There was a great disturbance at the studio at the time because they felt I should have been nominated for that show, but I was not. They were very upset about it."

When STAR TREK was canceled, Kelley's career momentum slowed considerably. Whereas Shatner and Nimoy continued to find regular acting work, Kelley didn't have is as easy. In the '70s he appeared infrequently on television, such as in an episode of the short-lived series THE COWBOYS as well as in the low budget horror film NIGHT OF THE LEPUS. Kelley wore a mustache for that role, almost as though he were trying to disguise himself.

When STAR TREK was revived as a Saturday morning animated series, Kelley was back in his familiar role of Dr. McCoy for the 18 episodes produced. But primarily Kelley worked the convention route in that decade, making an average of five thousand dollars per appearance at the numerous STAR TREK conventions which were popping up, and there were a lot of them. When STAR TREK was on the verge of being revived as a TV series in 1977, Kelley was signed for that and also signed up for the motion picture revival. His only screen work since the '70s has been in the STAR TREK movies, with one notable exception.

In the premiere episode of STAR TREK—THE NEXT GENERATION, Kelley appeared under heavy make-up as a 137 year old Dr. McCoy. The character is never named in the scene where he makes his cameo, but as he's being led along by Data, the old doctor is complaining about the Transporter, a device he still hates to use even after so many years.

DeForest Kelley is a fine actor who has rarely been given the opportunity to prove what he can do. Because of how easy he makes his role of Dr. McCoy appear, he isn't given his due nor is he considered for the more ambitious roles he'd like to play. At 73, Kelley is the oldest of the STAR TREK ensemble but STAR TREK VI—THE UNDISCOVERED COUNTRY ably demonstrated that he still has the strength and vigor that have always marked his performances.

CHAPTER 9

TALKING WITH THE GOOD DOC

It all started for De Kelly in Long Beach. He was with a Long Beach theater group for about three years. "It was quite a well known playhouse at the time and they used to be an old train depot up on Atlantic avenue, I believe, near Ocean, and that was converted into a very clever playhouse. There was the loading platform where everybody walked out during intermission and stood and talked, and that's where these plays originated. A number of people came out of there who went on to do quite well. But I started there and that's where the studio first saw me, and I ended up going to Paramount where I'm ending up now," he laughed. "I've come full circle.

"I had an uncle that lived in Long Beach," he explained as to how he came from his home in Georgia to California back then, "and he was a foreman for Shell Oil, but he was really a gambler. That was what staked him. So he said, 'You've never been out of the state of Georgia before, why don't you stay around a little longer?' I'd come out for 2 weeks. So I saw the ocean for the first time and it was very pretty then, very uncrowded. The old Riviara Hotel was still there looking like a castle and I just fell in love with the ocean. I got a job at an apartment hotel right across the street from the ocean so that I could just walk down the hill and go to the beach, and then I was doing plays at night."

When he was signed to do STAR TREK, this was something very new and different for Kelley. "I was never a science fiction fan so it was very strange to me. I had been doing a lot of other things, particularly westerns, and I'd gotten hung into 'heavy' roles which I'd done for about ten years. And when I saw the script it was just completely foreign. I'd never read much science fiction. I was never an aficionado of it like a lot of people. But I had done two pilot films for Gene Roddenberry, and when STAR TREK came along he wanted me for the doctor. Of course, he couldn't get me past the network because I'd always been doing the bad guy. They did that to you. They'd see you in one thing and associate you with that," Kelley explained.

GROOMED FOR McCOY

"Gene put me in a series where I portrayed a criminal lawyer out of San Francisco and his name was Jake Erlich. He was a very famous criminal lawyer, and we shot the whole thing in San Francisco. Again it was a little ahead of its time and it didn't sell. Then he put me in another one called POLICE STORY as a cop, and this was before the anthology series POLICE STORY. So I did that for him and then NBC saw it and decided that I could do the role, so I went in that door. But when I saw John Hoyt do it [in "The Menagerie"], he had this one scene with Jeffrey Hunter and I was very impressed with it. I thought if this character is developed well it could be very meaningful. And so I was pretty excited about it, but outside of the fact that I just thought it was seven weeks work, I thought that was that.

"I had just done a film at Paramount called WHERE LOVE HAS GONE with Betty Davis and Susan Hayward. Eddie Dmytryk directed it. I'd been doing these westerns, and I had done RAINTREE COUNTRY and WARLOCK and he said, 'I want to get you out of these westerns one of these days,' and when he called me for that, that was my move out of westerns. Then I went into STAR TREK and I thought,

well, that's seven weeks and it probably never will go any farther, and here I am 25 years later. Rather incredible."

After De Kelley had done a few episodes he began to get more interested in science fiction. "But it was rather foreign to me, the whole thing, and I just decided at that moment that I after I saw the nature of the stories that I would play this man as a man and not somebody that's far out. The appeal of STAR TREK to me was looking at a bunch of people going about a job in a very professional way in this very bizarre world, which is the way it looked to me. What intrigued me about it was that they all still had problems such as we have today, but in this bizarre world gave it kind of an oblique look of some sort. I thought it's down to earth, enlightening, compassionate, caring and that sort of thing. It might be fun. I don't know, I guess this worked. Sometimes it does, sometimes it doesn't."

AN ACCIDENT ON SET

Kelley revealed that the resuscitation scene in STAR TREK VI was the most physically involving medical sequence that he'd done in his 25 years with the series. "When I read the scene I knew it was going to be difficult to do. It was the first time I've ever asked a director to go to a set with me before we got on it. It was also interesting to me and appealing to me in the fact that all of the modern instruments didn't mean a damn thing, and he goes back to the old-fashioned way of trying to bring this man around. It was a very difficult scene to do and I felt it was a very important scene.

"We almost had a tragic accident, which no one will notice, but there was a huge lamp up above. When I was trying to bring David around and pulling these punches, this light exploded and the plate glass came down and just missed my neck and my shoulder and dropped so close to David's head that it was just a miracle that neither one of us were cut on the neck or his head split open. The light got so hot that the plate glass under the bulb exploded. After that they put another one in right away and we started again and I was back giving him this hit again.

In the course of it, my hand hit him and it busted my knuckles. The blood started to come out of my knuckles and I saw this blood drop before the hand came down and I forgot about pulling the punch and I hit David so hard on the chest that his eyes just popped open!" He laughed. "I really brought him around! They kept shooting it, but it was tragically funny."

BETWEEN KIRK AND SPOCK

In some respects Dr. McCoy was the comedy relief between Spock and Kirk, and Kelley explained what that position in the threesome was like. "I was kind of the catalyst for them. In the old shows I had a relationship with Kirk that was a different relationship. In the series he would sit down if he was in trouble and he'd be telling me his problems. He could tell me anything. It was also brought out that McCoy was the one man that could take him off the seat if he got out of hand. McCoy, I thought, was basically someone who had the feelings of a country doctor. He was compassionate and caring and that sort of thing, and emotional, and he looks at this man [Spock] who represents everything that he is not, and it was a source of irritation. But at the same time he would look at Spock and admire him. There was that underlying admiration. And there were the little moments that show up where you could tell that Spock admired the doctor. That's the way that thing developed. With that came certain remarks of course that were made along the line and were con-tinually added throughout the series.

"Now that we're all older I just try to work with the material. I don't try to hide anything. I kind of let it all hang out because the first thing the critics do, before we can ever read a review, we have to read the criticism of how we look, which is rather annoying. But I have learned to toss it aside now and get on with it, so I was kind of glad to do this movie so they can take a look at the way I really look. This is the way I look and I want you to know I've looked worse in other pictures I have done."

BETWEEN SHATNER AND NIMOY

Kelley was asked if sometimes he found himself in the middle in real life between the dynamic personalities of Leonard Nimoy and William Shatner when he was working in the films.

"Oh, very much, because they are, obviously, two stars, and I used to enjoy standing back, watching them. I've done that before with Kirk Douglas and Burt Lancaster. I'd never been an aggressive actor. I think that one of the secrets to an

actor performing well is not to be selfish. You're bet-ter when you're around better actors. The better the actor, the better you get, and some people are not that way at all. That probably hasn't helped my career any either, not being pushy, but I just can't do that sort of thing. But we all got along wonderfully well together.

"We have a lot of fun together. Bill can have a wonderful sense of humor, particularly on a set. It's hard to describe it, I can sit here and tell you, but he can be a very funny man, and like all of us, when he wants something he can let you know he wants that."

Kelley has appeared at many STAR TREK conventions in the past 20 years and was asked whether he's been able to determine from meeting the fans what kind of a need he thinks the series ful-fills in them?

"One thing is it seems to have brought a lot of people together who, in my opinion, would not have had a lot of friends or relationships otherwise. It provided a way of them getting to know each other who have something in common about this particular show that they love. It has afforded them an outlet artistically, and there are some very artistic people among them," Kelley observed.

STAR TREK IN RETROSPECT

"We have the largest university audience in the country. MENSA had a fan club for us for years. A lot of professional people who have been STAR TREK fans for years have come out of the closet and admitted it. They don't all have antennas. NASA are our biggest fans. During the series, Armstrong and all these guys sent me their picture and wanted my picture in return. So we sent all our pictures to the astronauts, and they ran the show in Houston on the big screen every Thursday night.

For the first 10 years at STAR TREK conventions, when we made an appearance, we always had an astronaut with us or somebody from NASA because we had the attention of the youth and they were trying to get youth involved with NASA. So we have some literate people that follow this show; very brilliant, bright people. A lot of talent out there."

Looking back over the 6 STAR TREK features, Kelley was asked how he views them in retrospect. "Well I know that number 2 was better than one. And 3 was okay. It was a good movie; not a bad film. And 4 was a real leap, a real good film. When I read the script I thought, this will make a good motion picture, period. Number 5, I had misgivings about going in, and I had a big deal with Harve Bennett about it, and I didn't

feel good about that script. This one [STAR TREK 6] I didn't really know. It played so much better than it read. It fooled me a little bit. It really did. It played better than it read to me, except for the story.

"Leonard had called me a couple of months beforehand and passed that story by me and asked me, what do you think of it? I said, I think it's perfect, and was very contemporary then. In the meantime a lot of other things have happened, and I thought, oh oh, we're going to lose it. All of this stuff is going to be gone by the time the film gets out there. Now the Gulf War and the Arabic nations have come about and so it's kind of made it a timely circle again. But as I said, it seemed to be like a steamroller because as we went on the film became more powerful, which is an unusual thing. I'm just hopeful that everybody will like it. Paramount and Leonard, and Bill and the rest of them that have seen it seem to be very proud of it."

THE FUTURE

Kelley commented on his fears after STAR TREK V. "I thought, that's it. We've done it. I really did. I thought that was the end. I had no conception that they would come around and do it again. Later on, after we sat around for a long while I thought, gee, it's the 25th year. It's a shame they're not going to do something. It's too bad. Then I started putting two and two together and I got to thinking about all the publicity that the studio could generate, and their commercialization they could do, and they have a residual audience out there if they like it. They won't go to see it if they don't like it. But this being the last film, they'll go see it. So even if they don't make a lot of money on it, it will all fall into place. Then I got to thinking, maybe they will. And they did."

It was important to him to do another film rather than go out with a disappointment like STAR TREK V. "That's the thing that pleased me. To go out with something that was worthy." But he readily admits that STAR TREK IV: THE VOYAGE HOME remains his favorite of the 6 features.

On the subject of Gene Roddenberry, Kelley was asked how he would rate Roddenberry as a producer.

"Gene had a down home, earthy quality about him. He was a big man. If you encountered him you would never dream the mind that he had. In a one-on-one conversation with him he could be as down to earth as possible until you started to engage him in some kind of philosophical discussion. Then suddenly this thing turns around! He was an intriguing human being, but he never sprung that brilliance until it was called upon. He just was a guy who loved life, loved to have fun. He loved to drink, he loved to eat. He loved women. He loved everything, and he was great fun to be with."

REMEMBERING GENE

On a more serious note, he dealt directly with the impact Gene Roddenberry and STAR TREK has had on all of the actors who starred in the series. "He changed the course of my life, and he changed the course of every life in this cast, whether they know it or not. Bill would not be who he is today, and Leonard would not be who he is today, and I wouldn't be sitting here and neither would anybody else [in the cast]. Not only that, but I know from certain mail, whether you agree with it or not, that he's also changed the lives of God knows how many thousands of other people. I think that he's a terrible loss and went out much too early." At the time of Roddenberry's death, DeForest Kelley was less than a year older than the creator of STAR TREK. "I'm 71, and I'm not ashamed to reveal it, I just hate to hear it!" he said, laughing. "And I hate it when they do these shows on TV: DeForest Kelley is 70 years old today! Get your cane, son!"

What will DeForest Kelley miss most about doing the STAR TREK motion pictures?

"Just knowing it's not there. It's been such a big part of my life for 25 years. Nothing has hit me yet. I will think more about it when someone says, this is it, period. Then you kind of take a breath and say, it's not going to be there. I wrote a poem that is really a comedy poem that I read when I make a personal appearance, and there are a couple of lines in it that I mention about STAR TREK. Something I always thought it would be; something constant such as the sea. It was like it was always going to be there, and it isn't always going to be there, but I think after the finality really hits I'll think about it and reflect on it."

HE'LL NEVER BE 137 AGAIN

Kelley had this to say about appearing on another NEXT GENERATION episode. "I have no intention of doing anything with them at all. I was supposed to be 137. I tried to talk them into just giving me a mustache and having him very distinguished looking, and maybe with a cane, and looking a hell of a lot better than that at a 137, and not going through those wig-fittings." Nimoy got off easy when Spock appeared. "He did it very lightly, yes. He says Vulcans don't age very fast." Kelley laughed. "He's got an answer for everything!"

Asked if there wouldn't always be a STAR TREK there to some degree, even if Kelley isn't making new films, he made some interesting observations about the possible future of THE NEXT GENERATION and may have even predicted the purpose of DEEP SPACE NINE, a project then unknown but not unanticipated.

"I would be inclined to think so. I know that THE NEXT GENERATION is becoming a terribly expensive show to do. I think the longevity of that show will depend upon the economics. And having done five years, then it's not impossible that they will pick up another cast for another generation. But I think that STAR TREK, or something relating to it, will be here long after we're gone. It'll pop up in some form somewhere, some way or another. I think it's become a phenomenal, fascinating kind of situation."

THE COMMUNICATOR

Nichelle Nichols   © 1991 Ortega/Ron Galella Ltd.

CHAPTER 10

OFFICER UHURA

by Jon S. Aiken

Of all the running characters on the original STAR TREK television series, Uhura was and is the most attractive of the bridge crew. As played by Nichelle Nichols, Uhura is a professional, experienced and extremely competent Star Fleet Communications Officer.

Granted that on the show she was not given as much screen time as many of us would have liked, but when she was on the screen all else seemed to fade into the background. Her presence was felt at all times on the bridge. Let's fact it, no matter what action Kirk wished to take against the antagonist of that episode, he couldn't tell anyone of his decision and actions without Uhura at her console. Yes, admittedly she grew very, very tired to opening and closing hailing frequencies, but it was a very vital task and it was best that it was in the most capable hands possible.

Uhura was a favorite during off-duty hours. She had a marvelous singing voice and in an over-computerized age where most all types of entertainment were "in a can," her live performances were much sought after.

As talented and beautiful as she was, her singing was known to get her into trouble on occasion. An excellent example of this occurred in the episode "The Changeling," The NOMAD computer had come onto the bridge and found Uhura humming as she went about her duties. NOMAD asked Uhura to explain the "noise" she was making. Uhura found the concept of trying to explain music, which to her is something very personal and emotional, to a non-feeling computer ludicrous. When she began to laugh at the whole idea, the computer zapped her and wiped her mind clean.

Thanks to advanced medical techniques of the 23rd Century, she was, of course, returned to normal. The moral, if there is any, I suppose is don't hum or laugh around your computer.

WOMEN IN THE 23RD CENTURY

The character of Uhura has only one point of controversy. This concerned one line of dialogue in the episode "City On The Edge of Forever." First, however, let us look at the women of Star Fleet in the 23rd Century.

Women of this time were considered the equal of men in the line of duty. Indeed, in the STAR TREK Writers' Guide, dated April 17, 1967, it states: "As with all female crewmen aboard, during duty hours she is treated co-equal with males of the same rank, and the same level of efficient performance is expected." A great deal was made of these facts when the show was originally aired. Uhura was a role model for young women. The "Libbers" of the '60s saw her as escaping the stereotypical "mother/secretary/fainting violet" syndrome women had been relegated to on national television.

As to the episode "The City On The Edge of Forever," Uhura, with Kirk, Spock, Scotty and assorted security men had gone down to the surface of the Guardian planet to look for McCoy. McCoy had gone insane due to an accidental overdose of medicine. Unknown to the rest of them, he had already gone through a time portal and changed the past.

When he changed history, the Enterprise disappeared.

There they all stood on the surface of a dead world. Their ship gone, their individual pasts gone or altered, no viable prospects of survival and Uhura uttered the phrase, "Captain, I'm afraid." Ms. Nichols got a good deal of mail about that, as if she wrote the line and volunteered to say it. Many female viewers felt this was an affront to the character and to women in general.

However, let's look at the general set-up of the show. Usually Kirk is the focal point. The difficult decisions fall to him; yea or nay, life or death, even perhaps ying vs. yang. As he is guided along the paths that enable him to make a decision he has with him his Greek chorus of Spock and McCoy. Their function is to point out the various solutions open to him, to show him the impact of what he faces.

Now, consider all of this in the light of the "City" episode. The Greek chorus there has been split up. McCoy has gone back in time and is not there to point out the human side, the emotional side if you will, of the situation they are facing. There is nothing to counterpoint Spock's non-emotional "computer" logic. She is not just speaking for herself, she is speaking for them all. In this role, she is not going against her feminism or against her character. She is right in step with it. Again and again, Uhura has been shown to be a vibrant and warm person who cares and feels for those around her. With her line, "I'm afraid," she was in keeping with this facet of Uhura's character.

NO DAMSEL IN DISTRESS

But, there was more to Uhura than the warm and feeling person. She was not above telling you were you could get off nor of telling you exactly what is what!

Being as skilled as she is in all forms of communication, it is not surprising that Uhura also mastered the technique of saying a great deal using very few words. One of the finest examples of this involved Uhura and it is also the genesis of one of my favorite lines in the series. It comes from the episode "The Naked Time." The crew of the Enterprise has been infected with a virus that not only allows, but forces, the individual to let down the barriers they have built up over the years as to their emotions and the fantasies that everyone has but would never admit to.

Sulu is one of the first to be infected. It seems his fantasy has always been to be one of the musketeers. As he dashes onto the bridge, his rapier flashing in the air, he grabs Uhura by the waist and cries, "Ah ha, me fair damsel." To which Uhura replies, "Sorry, neither!" and extricates herself from his grasp.

The viewer, and in this instance the reader, must stop a moment and think about all this line implies without actually saying it.

Uhura is stating that she is Black, she is proud of the fact and don't imply she is anything but Black. Secondly, she is saying that she is a normal, healthy woman with normal, healthy drives, which she has from time to time given in to but that didn't give Sulu the right to come putting his arms around her waist because she would decide who would do that!! Uhura was a woman who has indeed mastered communication when you consider how much she actually said with the two-word phrase, "Sorry, neither!"

AN AFRICAN OFFICER

As to Uhura's background, we know very little. According to the Writer's Guide, she was born in the United States of Africa. We know her name is Swahili and means "Freedom." She loves music and all it communicates. The series told us very little else about her. Nichelle states that she and Gene

Roddenberry worked out a background for Uhura in which the character came from Jahzeebo, Africa. Her language is Swahili. Her parents were physicists and professional people. Their expectations of her were high, so their expectations of her and their attitude toward her achieving this was no more than to be expected of her, even though they were proud of her.

Whatever her background, we can all agree that the show would have been less without her. She added variety, spice and dimension to a one-dimensional job. I for one hope she keeps opening hailing frequencies for a long, long time.

CHAPTER 11

THIS LADY COMMUNICATES: NICHELLE NICHOLS

Nichelle Nichols is secretive about her age, but she was born in Robbins, Illinois, near Chicago. In Robbins, Nichelle's father served as both the town Mayor and its chief magistrate. At the age of sixteen Nichelle wrote a ballet for a musical suite by Duke Ellington. She has studied in Chicago as well as in New York and Los Angeles. During her time in New York, she appeared at the famed Blue Angel and the Playboy Club. Between appearances at the clubs, she doubled as understudy to the lead in the Broadway musical "No Strings." She appeared in the title role of a Chicago stock company production of "Carmen Jones."

Nichols has demonstrated her ability as a performer by twice being nominated for the Sara Siddon Award as best actress of the year. She is an accomplished dancer and a beautiful singer. Her first nomination was for her portrayal of Hazel Sharp in "Kicks and Co.," the second for her performance in the hit play "The Blacks."

As vocalist with the Duke Ellington and Lionel Hampton bands, she toured throughout the United States, Canada and Europe. On the West Coast, Nichelle has appeared in "Roar of the Grease Paint, Smell of the Crowd," "For My People" and won high praises for her performance in the James Baldwin play "Blues for Mr. Charlie."

Nichelle was a relatively new face to television at the time of STAR TREK in the sixties, having previously appeared only in THE LIEUTENANT (which was also produced by Gene Roddenberry) and had the lead in an episode of CBS REPERTORY THEATRE. It was on THE LIEUTENANT that she was spotted by Gene Roddenberry. He remembered her and chose her for the role of Lt. Uhura when STAR TREK was picked up as a series, although she did not appear in either of the two STAR TREK pilots produced in 1964 & 1965. Nichelle has recently revealed that she had a brief affair with Roddenberry at the time she appeared on THE LIEUTENANT. Although the affair didn't last long, she and Gene remained close friends for many years.

THE LONG VOYAGE

"Producer Gene Coon demurs: 'I thought it would be ungallant to imperil a beautiful girl with 20-toed snaggle-toothed monsters from outer space.' But executive producer Gene Roddenberry is coming around: 'We're thinking about taking her down on the planets next season. Maybe we'll have wardrobe make her an appropriate costume for planet wear.'

"The canny Miss Nichols has already finagled an increase in her dialog quotient as communications officer. Her lines have run to such emotionless phrases as 'All hailing frequencies open, sir' or 'This frequency is open, Captain.' Once in exasperation she blurted out: 'Mr. Spock, if I have to say Hailing frequency open one more time, I'll blow my top! Why don't you tell me I'm a lovely young woman?' Her ad-lib improvisation was instantly incorporated in the script." So much for TV GUIDE's much vaunted accuracy as no such scene ever aired in any STAR TREK episode, unless it was in the Blooper Reel.

At the end of the first season of STAR TREK, Nichols was seriously considering leaving the series to pursue her singing career. But the weekend she was planning to quit, she met Martin Luther King at a fund raiser and he not only praised her success on the show but insisted that she was a vital role model for blacks in America. On STAR TREK she was treated as an equal by her comrades, something which was a new concept on television in the sixties. She reconsidered and told Roddenberry that she wouldn't be leaving the show after all.

Following the cancellation of STAR TREK, Nichols acting career has been spotty. She appeared in a few roles here and there, such as in the films MISTER BUDDWING, THREE FOR THE WEDDING, TRUCK TURNER, MADE IN PARIS, PORGY AND BESS (where she danced with Sammy Davis, Jr.) and DOCTOR, YOU'VE GOT TO BE KIDDING. But she got more work as a singer after STAR TREK than she did in TV and films. Nichelle also did the voice for Lt. Uhura on the STAR TREK animated series in 1974-75.

STAR TREK AND BEYOND

In 1969 Nichelle returned to the night club circuit after STAR TREK made what all believed would be its final voyage into rerun land. She'd previously had a great deal of experience from touring with Duke Ellington and the Lionel Hampton bands throughout the United States, Canada and Europe. When STAR TREK conventions started becoming popular in the '70s, Nichelle began making frequent appearances at them. On the strength of her continuing popularity in STAR TREK reruns, she released a single, "Shoop Shoop," on 20th Century Records and often sang at her many appearances at the fan conventions. She also released an album, "Dark Side of the Moon," through Americana Records. One of the songs she recorded is titled "Gene," a tribute to Gene Roddenberry done several years prior to his death.

In the '70s, NASA often sent representatives to the STAR TREK conventions, and through one of them she was invited to became involved with the space program. Nichelle flew aboard the C-141 Astronomy Observatory (which analyzed the atmospheres of Mars and Saturn), which was an eight hour, high altitude mission. She was also a special guest an the Jet Propulsion Laboratory in Pasadena on July 17, 1976 to view the Viking probe's soft landing on Mars. She wrote about the Viking mission for a publication of the National Space Institute. Nichelle joined the Space Shuttle astronaut recruitment program after giving a speech to the Board of Directors of the National Space Institute on "New Opportunities for the Humanization of Space," which dealt with the lack of women and minorities in the space program. Nichols, along with many of the other cast members from the original STAR TREK, attended the launching at Cape Canaveral of the first space shuttle, which was of course named The Enterprise.

Out of all the things she has been involved with, Nichelle points to her recruitment of minorities for NASA as being one of her proudest efforts. At least one of the astronauts on the ill-fated Challenger mission had been recruited by Nichelle.

During the eighties Nichols co-starred in the low-budget horror movie THE SUPERNATURALS. More recently she has been touring in a one-woman play wherein she portrays many of the famous black female singers of the twentieth century. During her leisure hours, Nichelle enjoys oil painting, designing her own clothes, reading science fiction, writing and sculpting. She has also acted as spokesperson for her favorite charity, "The Kwanza Foundation."

Nichelle has appeared in all six of the STAR TREK motion pictures and has written her memoirs, titled BEYOND UHURA, which will be published by Putnam Books in 1994. TV GUIDE reported that she was paid $450,000 for the tell-all book, in which she claims her brief fling with Gene Roddenberry wasn't as scandalous as some might lead you to believe.

CHAPTER 12

TALKING WITH
A GREAT COMMUNICATOR

Life at the end of STAR TREK as they knew it. That was much on the minds of people when Nichelle Nichols was interviewed on the impending release of STAR TREK VI—THE UNDISCOVERED COUNTRY.

It had to be asked. Everyone else was being asked then, if for no other reason than to see whether there was a consensus or a division of opinion on whether STAR TREK VI was indeed the final flight for the original and much revered cast of the starship Enterprise.

"It could be, and then again, who knows? I guess I feel like everybody else does. I've been on this press junket for the last week and the press is very excited about the film and everyone else who I know has seen it feels very strongly about it. They didn't know what to expect and came away very excited about it and would like for there to be another.

"I think the best ones that I liked of the film series are 2, 4 and 6. So I think what they ought to do is cancel 7 and go directly to 8! I stole that from Walter Koenig so you may hear him say it. I know the fans are going to be excited. They're going to love this movie. Perhaps there will be [another feature]. If not, this is a wonderful one to have ended the series of films with, and it won't bother me one way or the other. I've loved doing all the films. Each one is a miracle to me."

What still makes STAR TREK so popular after twenty-five years?

"It's really amazing that twenty-five years later the show is so popular that we all are still dedicated to giving the fans as much of ourselves as our careers will allow. It's sort of a wondrous, wonderful thing that people took to it so strongly and felt that this is the kind of future that they could subscribe to and wanted to believe in.

"You have to remember that we came at a time when the country was in a lot of turmoil. In the mid-sixties we were fighting for civil rights. We were fighting against the war in Vietnam. We were fighting against or opposing a third world war that could annihilate the whole world as we know it. And yet here was a program saying that not only did we not destroy ourselves in the 20th century but we made it into the 23rd century. And we not only made it but we made it in peace, that we had gotten our act together and were going forth in peaceful exploration," Nichelle explained.

OPTIMISTIC FUTURE

"I think one of the most important things about STAR TREK is that we talked about peaceful exploration. The very fact of the Berlin wall coming down, of Glasnost, of the two major powers talking to each other and expectation of peace, to me all comes out of what STAR TREK predicted in the '60s could be if men and women of good intentions could put aside their nationalism, their chauvinism, their reconciling themselves to a war every twenty years. They simply don't want to do that. They don't need to do that. There's got to be a greater plan and I think it's coming about now and I think we will have that 23rd century in a STAR TREK format and a STAR TREK kind of universe. I really hope so and I'm really proud to have been a part of it."

Is Nichelle surprised by STAR TREK's success?

"Well, I'm not now!" she said, laughing. "You know, hindsight is brilliant. I was surprised in a way that so many people took it on as a personal intent. I wasn't surprised at the show being popular because the show was so well written. Each show, each episode, would seem to be better than the last. And so, of course, they finally canceled it. But the people didn't cancel it. They refused to let it be canceled, and so here we are."

CRAFTING UHURA

When it comes to Uhura herself, how much of the character is Nichelle Nichols and how did that character come about?

"That's rather charming. It wasn't written in the original script. They sent for me from Europe and I came and interviewed against some of the top actresses who were up for it at the time. They had me read Mr. Spock's part because they hadn't written a part for Uhura. It wasn't even named yet. After I got the part, Gene Roddenberry and I got together and sat down and talked about the role. Where should she come from? Was she American? Who was she? Was she West Indian? And we really felt strongly that she should represent the United States of Africa to pull in the entire federation of Earth nations."

Since very few blacks were being cast in television shows in the early '60s, Nichelle could rightly be considered a pioneer in the industry, just as Martin Luther King told her one day.

"Well, I certainly was the first black female, if not the first black all together in a non-stereotypical role. It could have been cast by anyone so it was not a 'black' role as such. So in that way it was a pioneering moment in television history. It was a role of a woman who was a person with qualifications; to handle it, to be chosen, and it was these qualifications and characteristics and traits that I built her character on.

I first looked at what it would take. What kind of person would have been chosen? What were her qualifications? What were her characteristics? What was she like that qualified her to be chosen to go out on a five year mission as Chief Communications Officer of a starship, to go where no man or woman had gone before? What put her above everyone else for Captain Kirk to have chosen her as his Chief Communications officer? And that took on the framework for me to build her character.

"And so with talking to Gene we built a life for her. She comes from Africa and her language is Swahili. Her parents were physicists and professional people. Their expectations of her were high, so their expectations of her and their attitude toward her achieving this was no more than to be expected of her, even though they were proud of her. So we built this kind of thing, who she was and where she came from, not just being some actress cast and playing a role that she didn't know what she was doing. There was a purpose and there was a person and there was a life and blood and flesh and tradition behind her. Not only her family but her entire country, where she came from and her entire history."

IMAGE MAKER

Nichelle was asked about the story that she had originally planned to quit the television series after the first year. "I was very happy to have created a lovely character and being part of a wonderful show, but I only had that much experience, if you realize. I didn't have 25 years to look back and say, 'I can't leave this show.' But I was going to leave the show after the first year because I thought I'd created this wonderful character and now I want to go on and create some other wonderful characters.

I wanted to go back to live performances as well. I didn't really start out to be in television or films, although I was a dancer, a singer and an actor, my true love was theater. STAR TREK actually interrupted my career 25 years ago. I didn't fight against it, but it wasn't something I was just waiting for. So this came along and I was going to do other things. Also I felt that the show was so good, and each script was better than the last one that I said, 'This definitely is not going to last. They're going to cancel this!'

"Then as fate would have it, what happened was that very weekend that I told Gene Roddenberry that I was not going to continue with the show, I went to an NAACP fund raiser and I met Dr. Martin Luther King. Someone said, 'Nichelle, there's a big admirer of yours who wants to meet you.' And I looked around for a Trekker and there was Dr. King. I thanked him and he said, 'You know you're very important in our family. My children watch you, and my wife and I whenever I'm in on Friday nights. You have created such a wonderful role.' And I said thank you very much and I was talking and said that I was going to leave the show. He said, 'You cannot!' "And Dr. King said to me, 'You have created a role with such dignity and strength, and you have the first non-stereotypical role in television. This is not a black role and this is not a female role, and you've got them both, and this is vital and it's important because don't you see, more than just being a role model for black children or for our people, the world sees us now for the first time as we should be, and STAR TREK is doing that, and you have created that role. It's historic.' And he said, 'You've opened a door that can never be closed again, unless you abdicate. You've changed the face of television forever. We've got to keep it on because it's got to become second nature to people's vision and then they'll expect to see it. Don't you understand you're part of the command crew?!' I thought, wow, Dr. King is a Trekkie!

"I thought about it over the weekend and I went back and I told Gene that I've reconsidered and I told him why and he said, 'God bless Dr. King.' "

THE OTHER SIDE

What are the drawbacks of being so closely associated with a TV show like STAR TREK?

"It's a mixed blessing, of course. You create a very strong character and you're part of a show that has impacted so many people's lives in such positive ways and has become a phenomena in the history of television, that you can't help but get skewered to that role and recognized. It's different in that it's so popular and such a positive project. One of hope, adventure, and humanity. We did all of that without violating the first law of show business, and that's to entertain. That's the miracle of it because every show you've done has got a very strong, heavyweight message that coincides with our societal problems and mores of today. We're timeless."

But Nichelle was just one member of a multiracial cast and she readily admits that it wasn't an idea which was popular with everyone at the time. "They didn't even want the Vulcan because he was half-human. This nice human woman has been consorting with what? Green blooded, pointy-eared. . . "

And what about sex in STAR TREK? Why wasn't there more in the movies? "It's a given once it was established in the series that we were certain-

ly human and not evolved beyond that need, I think that it was just a given and it was then about doing a highly entertaining adventure with the cast and crew. I don't think there was really a need for it. I'm just surmising myself, but possibly they figured Captain Kirk had gone through the galaxy already!" she laughed, "and needed a break!" But then perhaps that's what it really meant when they said to go where no man has gone before. There is some seeming sexual tension between Spock and Valeris in STAR TREK VI, though, and Nichelle agreed that this is there. "Yes, there certainly is. And it was done so well."

ALMOST THE END

Regarding STAR TREK V and the problems the film encountered upon its release she observed, "I like five for a lot of reasons, but not nearly as much as four. For a lot of reasons we didn't get the pool of audience. One was the weakness of the script, and another is that we had a lot of competition that year with BATMAN and all of the others that came out."

One of the ideas discussed for STAR TREK VI was the much rumored academy days storyline, one which Nichols did not mince words about when it came to discussing that rejected script idea.

"I really didn't even want to consider that," she stated flatly. "I don't want to talk about it, but the fact of the matter is that Harve Bennett had an idea—and I felt it was a foolish idea because it demeans the show. It's one thing to do 'The Trouble With Tribbles.' It's one thing to do STAR TREK IV with whales where there's comedy, where there's amusement; but there's seriousness all the time. It's quite another thing to take the show and destroy its original concept for a buck, and I really don't think the buck will be there. From what I hear from fans, they'd hate it, and that pleased me because I cringed at the idea.

"I would have loved to have seen STAR TREK V turn over the helm to other people, younger people, and to have had something to do with bringing in younger people. Or to have had something to do with the next communications officer, who may or may not look like me but has to answer to me. I'd like to grow up and be a crotchety old communications head who gives them a hard time but has left high standards and be a legend in their eyes and they have to live up to that and answer to. I love that. And to

come back in a future STAR TREK or even to be referred to in subsequent STAR TREK films would just be a thrill to me. I don't have to be there. I don't have to do it, if you understand what I'm saying.

"The concept is very important to me and I think we'd make a very bad mistake trying to make STAR TREK something that it isn't when it certainly, successfully established itself as a serious, wonderful, marvelous program. We can take off from there and do all kinds of wonderful things with Gene Roddenberry's beautiful concept for the future."

SCOTTY AND UHURA

Something the future had never hinted at before was on display in STAR TREK V when Scotty professed his love for Lt. Uhura. A lot of people wondered where that came from.

"That was wonderful. It was fun. They didn't know what to do with that. They thought about a romance between Uhura and Scott and both Doohan and I said, 'That's impossible, that's ridiculous, that's crazy,' but what we did was look at each other and realize (at least this is what I did) that what was written on the page almost exactly mirrored the relationship between Jimmy Doohan and Nichelle Nichols," she explained. "Jimmy Doohan and I are always having a bit of a squabble over something or other; always friendly. Like over meeting for lunch. And then we would have a little argument, and then something could come up and of course we'd make up. And that's been the way it's been over the years.

"As a matter of fact, George Takei, and Wendy, Jimmy Doohan's wife, call Jimmy and me an old married couple," she said laughing, "who after twenty years love and adore each other but still wouldn't give up our battles with each other. So we played it that way.

I thought it was so charming that I didn't want to fight them and stop it. I knew the fans would go, 'WHAT? When did this happen?' And so that really is where I was coming from with it because in the scene, not only where he was ill, I thought, 'If anything ever happened to Jimmy Doohan I would absolutely die or I'd kill him if he goes and gets injured or sick! I'll never forgive him."

Her comment reminded her of Jimmy Doohan's heart problems of a few years before.

"As a matter of fact, when he was ill several years ago I flew in from some personal appearance and cut short my business to come back to L.A. so I could be there with him. I even told him in the hospital, 'If you don't get out of that bed I'll never forgive you!'

Jimmy and I have a very loving and long, deep, abiding friendship and I delighted in playing the role."

DANCE OF THE SEVEN VEILS

Nichelle had plenty to say about her little dance scene. "I am furious with them for not putting in the scene that set it up! The scene that set up the nude dance on the mountain top with the Sally Rand type fronds was that, when we landed and we knew these rag-tags were down below, we had to distract them so that Kirk and the guys could go down below and win the day. So originally, Kirk comes to me and says, 'Uhura, you will have to distract them while we go. . . ' And I said, 'But how?' And he says, 'You'll think of something!' And they're going, 'Captain, we've got to go now!' So I'm standing there watching them go and I'm going, 'Think of something. Hmmmm. I've always wanted to play to a captive audience.'

"So she thinks of something and the only thing she can think of, of course, to distract a bunch of rag-tag men that have been out in the desert for eons is to do her siren call. That's how that came about. I had a ball doing it. I loved it. As a matter of fact I went into training for it when I discovered what it was and what I had to do, and I had the two moons behind me. I loved it!"

MULTIPLE CONCLUSIONS

Since STAR TREK VI was supposed to be the last film, was there anything unusual about the last day of shooting? "We never had a last day of shooting. The last day of shooting we went right into a GOOD MORNING AMERICA interview on stage. We had all of the Champagne and food and so forth. Then we had a big photographic opportunity. Then the next day we had to come back and get in makeup and do a photo session. I guess the most poignant feeling was the first day. Going into VI with the understanding that it was definitely the last STAR TREK film was very emotional"

Then things started to happen as Paramount started wondering about what the ending should be and whether it should be dramatically changed. "Then the brass started coming in, and some of the shinier brass from New York started flying in. And then they started hearing about the dailies being so good, and so I guess they started getting excited. And the next thing you know we started getting rewrites and the ending was rewritten to give a more open ending." But she wouldn't say what the original ending had been before it was changed, although she did reveal that an early concept was to kill everyone off!

"I really objected to that idea, but that was only an idea. I said you don't have to blow us all to kingdom come just to not do it any more. Just don't do it any more! Leave Uhura alone! Even in giving one of the characters his own ship opens doors. George is in seventh heaven! I would love to really see them move on and expand, and then they could really get into some character development with Uhura back on Earth being the head of all communications. Then she could tell everybody where to go," Nichelle said, laughingly."

REAL STEPS

Part of Nichelle's non-STAR TREK activities have included doing recruiting for NASA, which she was very actively involved in during a crucial period when they were striving to expand their recruitment base.

"I became very interested in NASA and our space program in the middle '70s, when there was the largest STAR TREK convention ever. 40,000 people came to Chicago, which was my home town. It was the first time that all the stars of STAR TREK came together for it. It was wonderful. And NASA had seen fit to respond to the producers at the convention's request to send a scientist/representative to give a presentation on the long-range planning of the space program.

"I went to that presentation and was subsequently invited to NASA headquarters. I learned as much about our space program as possible. I was really fascinated with what we, as humans, had done since we stepped on the moon in '69 and where we were going. I wanted to make sure that I was represented, as a black, as a woman, as a mother, and as a person of the future. My delving into that caught NASA's attention because I began speaking to audiences. I was seeing thousands of people every week from the STAR TREK conventions and other personal appearances, and I was talking about NASA and where we are going and how we have a responsibility to it."

In 1978 when NASA was about to recruit the first astronauts for the space shuttle program, they called in Nichelle for consultation.

"I had several contracts with them on youth-oriented programs, but now they called me in on a consultation to a system in recruiting the first women and minority astronauts for the space shuttle. That would be the first time that women and minorities would really be taken seriously as applicants. I took off from my career for the next six months and personally traveled all around the country, speaking at universities and professional organizations like the organization of black physi-

cists and engineers. I even went to the aerospace industry to convince qualified people that NASA was serious."

COALITION

Nichelle continued; "They understood the historic moment and many applied who had never considered going into space as a career. And some who really were interested, who really wanted to go but did not want to apply and be rejected out of hand simply because they were female or black or a minority. The response was tremendous over that last four months of recruitment and for the next two months until I turned in my report. When NASA came to me they were already underway about seven months and they only had about a hundred applications from women, none of which were qualified for what they were looking for in the sciences and engineering. Only about 35 minorities across the board had applied. Although they were doctors, lawyers, and engineers, they were unqualified in the areas NASA were looking for.

"When I finished, exactly 1649 women had applied. I went on television, I went on radio, I did public service announcements. I really did a media blitz to convince women, to convince black people and other minorities that this was the moment in history in which they absolutely must answer. The response was very rewarding. NASA received so many qualified people that they raised the recruitment core minimum from thirty to forty. Whereas they were looking for one woman, maybe. One black man, whatever, that hopefully they would find to change the tide of history and change that tapestry of the all-white male astronaut corp. I gave them so many qualified people that they chose six women, three black men, one Asian and subsequently recruited people from that list for subsequent recruitment drives. It's very prideful."

THE MANY WORLDS

STAR TREK fans are often stereotyped as being nerdish outsiders, but Nichelle disagrees with that characterization. "I think some nerds brought that up. Trek fans come in all shapes and fashions. With anything that's popular, I think you're going to get a fanatical fringe element, but most of the fans that I've encountered are probably some of the most intelligent people I've ever met, with a great sense of humor. They know what they're doing when they come to a STAR TREK convention on the weekend, and they celebrate. They get away from work and away from mundane problems of everyday life. Some of them like to dress up like the characters. They share their thoughts about the characters, get to see the blooper reels and lots of films. And they really love to make the costumes. It's not go out and buy the costumes, but how true you can come to creating it. I saw a Klingon costume on a girl just this weekend that was as close to anything in Hollywood. There's been some thefts and I asked her where'd she get that? And she said, 'I made it,' and she opened it up to show me her workmanship, and sure enough, she had made it."

Regarding the characters on STAR TREK, she was asked why none of them have been presented as having families of their own? "I think when you're talking about charting galaxies there's not much time for the home front by the fire. I think that Gene very wisely made some adjustments with THE NEXT GENERATION in which you have young people and a son of one of the characters. You can think of a 5 year mission and putting your life on hold because it's not just a hop, skip and a jump when you're traveling a few light years. But then the phenomena happened with STAR TREK of the fans that would not let it die over the years."

The subject became a bit more serious when Nichelle was asked about Gene Roddenberry, who had died just the month before this interview.

"He was a wonderful, beautiful man. I loved this man, very much. Very deeply. I've known Gene for over 30 years. Before STAR TREK he gave me my first episodic TV job and with an introductory guest star billing. It was in THE LIEUTENANT. It shows you how the man was. If he likes your work he never forgets a friend. Three years later when he was doing STAR TREK he insisted that they bring me back from Europe to do the show, and I'm real glad he did."

THE STAGE LIGHTS BECKON

So far as life after STAR TREK VI is concerned, Nichols wasn't that certain that she'd really be up to doing any more movies because she's managed to find that there is indeed life after STAR TREK.

"I'm really back into my career, which is more than a communications officer on a starship. I'm very proud of that character that I was given the opportunity to create and I love the concept of the show. I love the characters of the show. I love Captain Kirk, I love Mr. Spock, I love Scotty, I love Sulu, and I love Chekov and Nurse Chapel. I guess it's just a point in time where you really have to go on, and my music career, and my show 'Reflections' and I have a destiny of our own.

"You know, you make plans in life and I don't think anyone's life goes exactly as planned. I started out as an actress, singer, dancer and in the musical theater. That was my life. I've had an exciting and wonderful life that is no place near what I thought it would be. I saw myself on Broadway and maybe making films later, but as a Broadway musical-comedy star. I thought that would be my life. When I got STAR TREK I thought it was simply a stepping stone and that I would go on to other things, and what a wonderful big step that certainly was. It was one of the terrific things that happened to me. But I thought I would go on to many other things.

"I didn't realize that my interests are so vast that one career probably couldn't encompass everything. I love my work and I love having created Uhura. So it's not something I regret, but it has enhanced everything I've done as a writer, as a speaker, as a performing artist. But you see, I've come full circle and here I am, where I began, where I love it the most—in musical-comedy, and that's exciting for me."

[This chapter also includes material culled from a second interview with Nichelle Nichols conducted by Michael Ruff on May 5th 1990.]

THE ENGINEER

James Doohan   © 1988 Smeal/Ron Galella Ltd.

CHAPTER 13

CHIEF ENGINEER "SCOTTY"

Ever since he was a "wee lad," as his father Ian called him, Montgomery Scott was always tinkering with something. Montgomery grew up on a sheep farm outside of Aberdeen, Scotland. As a child, Montgomery had three favorite pastimes: playing with the family's big sheep dog, Duke, fixing things and watching other people fix things.

After Montgomery was born, Duke more and more became the boy's pet rather than the family sheep dog, and Duke would follow Montgomery wherever the boy went. As a very young boy, Montgomery would run in the fields with Duke, trying to ride the dog, making up complex adventures. As Montgomery got older, Duke began to follow him to school, and waited for him at the end of the day.

After school, Montgomery tinkered out in the shed. He started with simple mechanical farm implements, taking them apart one piece at a time, studying each component, what they did separately, and what they did as part of the whole. Then he would put them back together. Duke often sat up in one corner to watch Montgomery work, and Montgomery enjoyed the audience.

As he got a little older, Montgomery started working on larger things, like computers and his father's hovercraft. Montgomery was quite patient. If he couldn't figure something out immediately, he might curse and bellow a bit in frustration, but he would let it sit and mull it over in his mind and go back to it later. He was talented and could figure out most gadgets relatively easily. Soon Montgomery was getting the bulk of his education by himself. He learned advanced physics concepts, mathematical theory and the origins of logic long before his classmates. He augmented his practical work out in the shed with curiosity-satisfying trips to the Aberdeen library to put the ideas into perspective.

MUSIC AND ELECTRICITY

It came as little surprise to his family that Montgomery did well in school, and exceptionally well in math and the theoretical sciences. He also showed an interest in ancient Gaelic culture, picking up a set of bagpipes for his fifteenth birthday. In his spare time, Montgomery practiced the bagpipes while reading vidisplays of technical manuals.

Montgomery joined the Aberdeen Marching Band, playing the bagpipes. The band played all over the Earth and the Federation for various state ceremonies and parades. Ian and Montgomery's mother Mary were proud of their son, although Ian almost had a heart attack the day he went out to find his son puttering with the farm's private generator. Montgomery stood in the middle of enough current to turn his tartan kilt black. Ian found Montgomery upgrading the generator to produce a cleaner power flow.

Although Montgomery spent much of his time buried in technical pursuits, he also found plenty of occasion for old-fashioned carousing. He would go out with his friends, Duncan, Sean, and Alan and head into Aberdeen after school. Ian passed down the secrets of distillery to his son, and Montgomery kept a still in his work shed. The boys always went into town with a bottle or two of good quality family Scotch. Once in town they picked up a female or two a piece and would joyride in Duncan's hovercar. Montgomery beguiled many a woman with winning charm. Too free-spirited to hang on to one particular lass, he enjoyed chasing several.

Montgomery dreamed of adventure, but fell in love with generators and computer systems. He loved them more than any woman he knew in Aberdeen. Because of his high scores on math and physics aptitude tests, Montgomery was offered scholarships to many engineering universities sponsored by astroflight corporations with high paying development positions available to him upon graduation.

ENGINEERING HIS FUTURE

Montgomery was familiar with commercial spaceflight, and the "piddling developments" that were made there, as he put it. "Those clunkers couldn't get out of molasses for anything," Montgomery said. He wanted to be where the real challenges lay, in Starfleet. Starfleet was then embarking on an aggressive development plan for a series of new heavy cruisers that would go faster for longer periods of time than any other in history. "Those lassies'll really go places," Montgomery said.

Upon entrance into Starfleet Academy, Montgomery sank into any and all available manuals on Starfleet technology, including plans for the new Constitution class ships. "Smoother than a shot of old Scotch," Montgomery said in his best brogue.

His classmates were fascinated with the new Scottish cadet who wore his lucky kilt to exams. The women loved his honey-warm brogue, and listened to him spin yarns of the Scottish highlands for hours. All the cadets eagerly noted Montgomery's age-old recipe for Scotch, which the engineering cadets happily used to improve the quality of their "engine-room hooch," crude moonshine that Montgomery's recipe and expert touch made so much better. The cadets also loved Montgomery's exciting flair for the Scottish ways, and nicknamed the friendly chap "Scotty." Whether it was a class taught by the Academy's most pedantic instructor, or a night pass into San Francisco, Scotty made sure he enlivened it for his peers. They all became his friends, Scotty took his engineering seriously, but took the engineer with a grain of salt.

In his last year at Academy, Scotty opted for advanced engineering work on the Constitution ships, eventually contributing the dilithium flow design to the plans. For his exceptional work as a cadet, the dean of engineering commended Scotty by sponsoring him for a promotion to full ensign, and ordered that Scotty's cadet cruise would be to help supervise the Constitution's shakedown cruise.

SPACE TREK

For two years he was aboard for the full shakedown, a year longer than traditional cadet cruises. Scotty watched every systems monitor aboard ship, especially tending to the dilithium, fiddling with his original plans occasionally, retooling the cut of the crystals for maximum efficiency for such a large ship that ran a huge number of systems. Scotty loved feeling he had contributed something. He learned that if he wasn't constantly on demand to produce a hundred different engineering miracles at once, he felt useless, which he hated.

Scotty didn't get much of the adventure he had dreamed of as a child because Starfleet didn't completely trust the new ship, yet. But he was eventually given the chance to proudly say that with only a few minor reworkings, Constitution and her sisters were the best the Federation had. Scotty felt a warm spot when he realized he was lumped in with the distinguished Federation minds.

After the Constitution mission, Starfleet offered to let Scotty remain with the Constitution to supervise a minor refit, then ship out with her again. Parts of the Constitution had already slipped into near-obsolescence. The state-of-the-art at that very moment was the glistening new Enterprise.

The Enterprise had just completed a scaled-down version of the Constitution shakedown under Captain Robert April who was moving on to the Federation diplomatic corps. Captain Christopher Pike was taking over as commander for a full five year mission. This was the chance for Montgomery Scott to not only serve aboard the most current advanced ship, but to enter actual deep space. Scotty beamed at the opportunity for a little starhopping adventure.

ADVENTURE

He transferred on as assistant chief engineering officer, lieutenant junior grade. The Enterprise made Scotty even prouder than the Constitution. The Enterprise was one of those rare ships with personality. "From Day One, she was a gallant lady," said Scotty later in life. Scotty served two five year missions under Pike, followed by a six month refit he supervised when his chief engineering officer went on maternity leave.

She resigned from the service before the second five year cruise, and Scotty then served under Clegg Pitcairn, an old engineer who had been one of the supervisors of the Constitution design team. After the second five years, which included the infamous Talos incident, Commander Pitcairn went into retirement.

Once again, Scotty supervised a refit, but this time in his own right, as he had been promoted from lieutenant commander and given the job of chief engineer. "Accepting that promotion was a true marriage to the Enterprise. It was sick or poor, 'til death do us part. And that's how it was," Scotty recalled.

With the promotion and refit came a mostly new crew. Pike and his exec, Number One, were gone. Captain James T. Kirk came aboard as skipper. Scotty sized him up as another man who loved his ship, and true to his belief, Kirk never asked more from the old girl than she could give.

Scotty had found that too many people think of starships as pieces of technology to bully around. To Scotty, the Enterprise was different. Treat her with care and she'll look after you forever.

Many years later, after the crew of the Enterprise began going their separate ways, Scotty found himself exploring a remote planetoid where his ship crashed. With chance of rescue anytime soon remote, he and another crewman put themselves into a Transporter loop, from which only Scotty survived to be rescued 75 years later by the Enterprise-D. With a new universe to explore, Scotty felt that his life had started over again in more ways than one.

CHAPTER 14

SAILING WITH GENE: JAMES DOOHAN

Like William Shatner, James Doohan is Canadian by birth and is a native of Vancouver, British Columbia. During World War Two Doohan earned the name "bad boy" while flying an artillery observation plane for the Royal Canadian Air Force. Regarding those days, Doohan says, "I guess they thought I was crazy because I used to fly my plane on a slalom course through rows of telephone poles." Prior to this he had been wounded in battle on D-Day.

Following his discharge from the military, Doohan decided to use the scholarship he had coming to return to school. But shortly after starting college he was listening to the radio one night and was appalled at the level of professionalism he heard, believing that he could do much better himself. Chance brought a brochure his way on training for a career in radio, and he followed up on it. Doohan eventually became one of the busiest voice artists in the medium.

The actor originally came to the United States in 1946 on a two-year scholarship to the Neighborhood Playhouse in New York City. James Doohan continued on there as a teacher for three more years, instructing his students in acting techniques at New York City's Neighborhood Playhouse. In 1953 he returned to Toronto, Canada, where he lived for the next eight years. During this time he appeared in more than four hundred live and taped television shows, numerous motion pictures and plays, as well as over three thousand radio shows. He was clearly one of the busiest performers in the business.

In the sixties, Doohan became a very busy working actor, particularly on television where he appeared on such shows as BONANZA, HAZEL, THE VIRGINIAN, BLUE LIGHT, DANIEL BOONE, THE F.B.I., THE GAL-

LANT MEN, GUNSMOKE, HAZEL, THE MAN FROM U.N.C.L.E., THE OUTER LIMITS, PEYTON PLACE, RETURN TO PEYTON PLACE, SHENANDOAH, THEN CAME BRONSON, THE TWILIGHT ZONE, VOYAGE TO THE BOTTOM OF THE SEA, THE FUGITIVE, IRON HORSE, BEN CASEY, and BEWITCHED.

A BURDEN AND A BLESSING

In 1966 he tried out for recurring roles on both VOYAGE TO THE BOTTOM OF THE SEA and STAR TREK. Although he was offered the role of Chief Sharkey on VOYAGE first, he turned it down. Shortly thereafter he was invited to join the permanent cast of STAR TREK. Doohan gained a mastery of dialect and voices while working in radio, although the Scottish accent employed on STAR TREK has succeeded in typecasting him in the eyes of Hollywood. Even when he has gotten an infrequently offered guest shot on a TV show, he's tended to be asked to play a Scot, such as he did in an episode of MAGNUM P.I. with Tom Selleck.

On November 22, 1967, Doohan married his second wife, the former Anita Yagel, a secretary employed by Paramount whom he met in the studio commissary. He has four children by a previous marriage.

Among his many motion picture credits are THE WHEELER DEALERS, FELLOWSHIP, JIGSAW THE SATAN BUG, BUS RILEY'S BACK IN TOWN, PRETTY MAIDS ALL IN A ROW and MAN IN THE WILDERNESS. He also appeared in several films produced by the National Film Board of Canada.

An accomplished carpenter and wood carver, James Doohan has made several pieces of furniture which the Doohans use in their Hollywood Hills residence.

When STAR TREK was revived in 1974 as a Saturday morning cartoon show, Doohan provided his voice not only for Scotty, but also for several other characters, such as in the episode "Yesteryear" where he was the voice of The Guardian and of Spock's father. After STAR TREK he secured a recurring role on JASON OF STAR COMMAND in 1978-79 while doing additional voice work on various animated series.

LIVING A STAR TREK LIFE

Doohan has appeared in all six of the STAR TREK feature films and joined the elite group of original Trek actors who have appeared on THE NEXT GENERATION. In season six of TNG, James Doohan reprised his role of Scotty in the episode "Relics." The show even includes a touch scene where Scotty visits the holodeck and recreates the original bridge of the starship Enterprise as it appeared in the days of the 1966 television series.

Beginning in the seventies, Doohan has become a regular fixture at STAR TREK conventions, appearing at them all over the world, including in England and Australia. In the late eighties he suffered a heart attack but has fully recovered and gone on to maintain a fully schedule of activities.

Seeing how much money Paramount continues to earn from STAR TREK, including the use of his character, Doohan has decided to go after some of that for himself and has been working on his autobiography since 1991. Although he was originally thinking of publishing it himself to sell directly to the fans at conventions, Doohan has since struck a deal with Pocket Books and his yet untitled memoirs will be published in late 1994.

CHAPTER 15

TALKING ENGINES

Out of all the actors closely identified with STAR TREK over the years, no one knew Gene Roddenberry better than James Doohan. It's interesting that James Doohan should wind up becoming famous for his work as an actor because he'd never intended to have a career in acting.

"I never thought about it at all. I had no thought of ever being an actor. It all kind of gushed on to me by my own personality and fate. I was 19 and the war came along, and in Canada that meant the third of September 1939. I spent six years and two months in the army and five and a half of that was overseas. So when it comes down to veteran's benefits, boy I had it in spades when I was discharged. They owed me nine years of university training. I came home and stayed around for about a week, went up north fishing for about a week; came back wondering what the heck I was going to do. One of my older brothers said why don't you go and take the Veterans Administration school and bone up on academic subjects and then you could get into Western in the middle of February of '46. I had no idea what I wanted to do but I certainly hadn't had a lot of subjects for the past six and a half years even though I went from a private up to a captain. I went to the British officer's school in England. That was great training. I trained a lot of people for the invasion of Normandy and darned if I wasn't number one off on my beach! I was wounded that night.

"So I went to the school and had been there about four or five weeks between Christmas and New Years of '45/'46. I happened to take a break from studying and I turned on the radio, and it was bad. It was so bad. I just couldn't believe how bad it was. I got something together to read and nine o'clock the next morning I went down to the local radio station to make a transcription and then I listened to it. I'd never heard my own voice before. I said to the operator, God that's awful! And he said, 'I don't think it's awful at all.' Okay, where do you go to learn?"

DESTINED TO PERFORM

Doohan smiled and said, "This is where fate comes in or happenstance or God or whatever. In that mail delivery that morning, before I did the transcription, there was a brochure of a drama school opening in Toronto. I sent them a telegram—got an answer back. I was there the following Monday. Six months later I had won the top scholarship, which was two years free tuition at the Neighborhood Playhouse in New York City. Then when I finished there they asked me to stay on and teach, which I did for about three years. But by that time I was already into live television. I had already done fifteen plays. Five and a half years later what else did I know except acting—and artillery.

"I was told by my instructor in the neighborhood playhouse that it would take me 20 years to become a full actor and after I'd been an actor about 19 years I began to feel exactly what he was talking about. There isn't anything I can't do. Just ask me and I'll do it because my acting ego is unbelievable. When you know that you have done the work, and a reviewer says, 'James Doohan was superb.' It's not false ego at all! You just say, 'Hey,

you're damn right!' I work for it. That's different. That's not phony!"

Discussing his extensive history of doing voice work, Doohan remarked that the first time he did a Scottish accent was in an episode of HAZEL. STAR TREK was the second time. There isn't an accent that I can't do if I can hear it, because I really have that kind of an ear and I've been doing it ever since I can remember, since I was 5 or 6 years old. My mother tells me that I would read out loud, maybe 6 or 7 years of age, and I'd walk from the living room to the hallway to the kitchen to the dining room to the living room to the hallway and every time I'd go through a doorway I would change my accent. So accents are also not commercial though I love to do them, just for the heck of it."

AN ACCENT ON ACTING

Doohan has also had to create some accents on occasion. "There was a producer of radio in the CBC in Toronto that I had never worked for. His name was Frank Willis. He was a very conservative guy and I'd just say 'Hello, Frank.' When I'd been there two or three years, he called me one day and he said, 'Jim, can you do a Persian accent?' I said, 'Sure, Frank.' Who the hell knew what a Persian accent was? Who had heard one? There was no videotape then. No great news broadcast from around the world. So I got the job and all I did was a cross between an Indian from India and a Greek, and now I can't even remember what the accent sounded like but it damn well sounded like a Persian to me! And at the end he said, 'Boy, how do you do it?!' I said, 'Talent, Frank.'

"Then very shortly after I arrived in Toronto there was a Swedish director there, a Canadian Swede named S.A. Ljungh, and he was a great character director. He was doing a two hour show, non-commercial for the United Nations and he said to me, 'Can you maybe do a Hitler?' I said that I think I could do a pretty fair job, but he was doubtful. I just fiddled around with it a little bit, but on dress rehearsal I really gave it to him and I talked exactly like Hitler, only in English. And from that day on I worked on every show that he had. It's no wonder I did 4,000 radio shows in eight years."

When asked whether he was still surprised to encounter people who didn't realize that the accent was a fake, he explained, "They've already typecast you. I can remember after we stopped shooting STAR TREK, I got a play in 1973 in San Francisco playing one of the leads as a British barrister. In fact from that part I got one of the best reviews that I ever got in my life and I always got good reviews. I had Scottsmen come backstage afterwards and say, 'God, laddie, I thought you were a real Scot! You do it right, though!' and they were proud of that, which is fabulous. I don't do them unless I do them right.

"I've been in their living room as a Scottsman thousands of times and that's the only way they can look at you. They know it but they're never disappointed because they love me anyway. That's the beautiful thing about it. I have a great rapport with the audience and I just love them."

DOOHAN = SCOTTY

What has James Doohan gotten from Scotty? Leonard Nimoy has spoken of really liking Spock and learning a lot from him, as an example.

"I can tell that," Doohan agreed. "I know that Leonard has learned a lot from Spock, even as a person. Even though he has always been a terrific guy, he has become wiser. And is acting wiser. He probably didn't mention this, but in the animated shows, Leonard refused to be in the show at all unless Uhura and Chekov were brought in, because they were not scheduled to be in it. Just McCoy, Kirk, Spock and myself. So he just told Paramount no. I won't be in it until you get them in it."

Regarding Scotty, is the Chief Engineer of the Enterprise a character he likes personally? "Yeah, I like him because I kind of like myself and he's 99% James Doohan and one percent accent."

On the subject of Gene Roddenberry James Doohan was quite open and expansive with what he had to say.

"A couple of times Gene came to me and said, 'Jimmy, don't make the accent too thick.' And the fans said that there were a couple of words I said in one of the shows and there was no accent there. I said, well, that was probably because Gene had just finished telling me don't make the accent too thick."

HIS FRIEND GENE

Out of all the actors who worked on STAR TREK, Doohan perhaps knew Gene Roddenberry best. "Gene and I would go sailing a lot and he was one hell of a navigator. We were fogged in on Santa Rosa island, which is about 50 miles away from Santa Barbara harbor, and I said, well you set the course and I'll handle the boat. So he said, 'Okay, take this heading here.' We arrived within about 50 yards of the harbor.

"Engineering wise he wasn't so hot. There was a day that looked as if it was going to be a very calm day and we headed out from the marina and I said let's stop and get some gas. 'Oh, no,' he says, 'let's not take that time. We'll be okay.' So we got about a mile out and we were crawling along at a quarter of a knot an hour and it was terrible. It would have taken us forever to get to Catalina over to Avalon. So we started up the motor and about ten or fifteen minutes later the motor stopped. So at nine o'clock at night we limped in to Avalon harbor doing a knot an hour, I suppose. Gene called over to San Pedro and flew a mechanic over and the mechanic checked the motor and said, 'You're out of gas.' I said, 'Gene, let me handle the engineering.' But we got along well together."

And the controversy continued in those days leading up to the imminent release of STAR TREK VI—THE UNDISCOVERED COUNTRY. Was it the last voyage on the Enterprise for the original crew? Votes were being tabulated. . .

"There's no way at all that this is going to be the last because this film we've just done is a perfect film. Absolutely flawless and there's no reason at all it won't make probably $150 million, and Paramount is not going to turn that down. So there. I don't care what Bill [Shatner] says. He's going along with the house ruling on that. It's all a big ploy." Although Shatner did say that if asked he would return, as would Doohan. "Absolutely! Good God almighty! To do our role again. Good God, why wouldn't we come back?"

And what is it that he likes about being involved with STAR TREK?

"Mostly meeting all the gorgeous fans, because they've asked me the same question, and I say you are the reason. I just got back from Australia and I was adored in Australia. I did two conventions there. One in Perth and one in Brisbane. And they just treat you like a god! Really special! That's the way I get treated everywhere."

RATES TREK

What's the most unusual place that he's been recognized? "I did a convention in Germany in August and I stopped off in Heathrow to change planes and I heard this hustle and bustle behind me.

Two young fellas came dashing in front of me, and they had semi-dark skin and they said, 'It's Scotty! STAR TREK! Yeah, yeah!' About fifteen of them all came up and I said, 'Where are you from?' Malaysia.

"We're all over the world, in 54 different countries. I've met the guy who does my voice in German. And I have a picture of the guy who does my voice in Japanese."

Out of the six STAR TREK feature films he appeared in, Doohan said that he regarded THE UNDISCOVERED COUNTRY as his favorite of the movies and was quite willing to analyze the previous films in the series.

"Number one got very boring to get to V'ger. It took them 12 minutes to get to V'ger and all they showed us was thin white clouds. It was terrible. At the preview in Washington, Bill Shatner and I fell asleep.

"In THE WRATH OF KHAN the editing was lousy, except for what the director had edited in the ABC version. The TV version was much better. My part was slashed to bits and I think I know who to blame for that but I can't mention his name." One of Doohan's objections to the editing involved the Ike Eisenman character who was Scotty's nephew, but all references to that were expunged from the theatrical version. "Crazy kind of editing! It was just bad.

But that's all included in the ABC version and I just found out that Nicholas Meyer was the guy who edited the ABC version."

Regarding STAR TREK III: THE SEARCH FOR SPOCK, Doohan observed that the film had, "A so-so script. Number four was a great story and everything else but not pure STAR TREK. Number five was just a bad film. Number six is perfect; flawless.

"To me the perfectly edited WRATH OF KHAN was perfect STAR TREK and number six is just absolutely sensational. It's got suspense, it's got content. As a matter of fact people are going to have to go and see it three times just to catch everything. I had guests there [at the screening] and they said, 'Gee, I'm going to have to see it again! I missed this and I missed that.' I know very well that's going to happen." And Doohan credits all that to director Nicholas Meyer. "Oh yes, because he also wrote it. He and David Flynn wrote it. I like Nicholas Meyer! He really knows what he's doing."

MAKING VI

On how filming STAR TREK VI was compared to working on the other motion pictures in the series, the actor said that it wasn't that difficult and, like most of the others, it was mostly shot in California. "It wasn't rigorous for me. It was rigorous for Bill and Leonard and Kelley, but not particularly for us. They had to shoot everything there at night on the planet."

Did James Doohan ever imagine in 1966 that he'd be interviewed 25 years later about his latest appearance in STAR TREK?

"Oh God no! Nobody anywhere could come close to imagining this sort of thing happening. It's one of the biggest publicity things in town! It's just sensational. I do about 150 interviews a year mostly sitting in my good chair for radio around the country because I do a lot of these conventions all over. I'm even scheduled for my third celebrity of the week in Disneyworld, so that's fun."

And yet his role as Scotty on STAR TREK did lead to typecasting for the actor and limited his opportunities after the original TV series had been canceled.

"Absolutely. No doubt about it. What I trained myself for in the first 20 years, I have really not been allowed to do since I've been typecast." And while it bothers him the benefits derived from the ongoing interest in the TV series over the years has also helped to offset those drawbacks. "It would really bother me very much if I didn't make a living from STAR TREK, and I do make a living. I make way over six figures in personal appearances alone and that'll go on for quite a long while. When it comes right down to it, I've probably personally only seen about a million people. There are all sorts of other people out there and the people at conventions are increasing by fabulous numbers. I've asked the question the past three or four years—how many are at their first STAR TREK convention? The minimum reaction is 85%."

THE SECRET OF TREK?

What draws people to the conventions to meet the stars of the various forms of STAR TREK? What makes someone a Trekkie while someone else is not?

"I don't think anybody knows that. I think that STAR TREK the series just had some kind of magic to it. I don't think it can be described any other way. I don't think any other answer, such as good writing, terrific idea in the first place, the fact that it's space, that it gives hope for the future—I don't think that's enough to satisfy people. It just has some kind of magnetic drawing that has even created a new series, which a lot of people like but a lot of people don't like. And it's created all these movies, and hopefully every movie is a great one that's full of all sorts of magic. I have no idea really, but when you find that much love you better go along with it."

So Doohan is definitely glad to be a part of the 25 year experience and isn't at all sorry that Scotty became so popular?

"Not really. How can I be sorry when you're sort of known and loved throughout the world? Hey, it means an awful lot to me, loved as much as we are. I get letters from all over the world. People in New Zealand knit me socks. I get artifacts from Japan. I get perfume from Brazil, and so on. It's really quite fascinating. It's also become another life, completely different than what I would have imagined. I would still be an actor struggling for parts. But if I had kept on doing the kinds of parts that I was doing in different shows before STAR TREK came along, and ever since television started, I would hope that I would end up, if things had been different, in the kind of parts that Jack Nicholson would play. Maybe I'm daydreaming, but I did every kind of part before, so why shouldn't I do that sort of part in the future? But being typecast sort of stopped all that."

THAT OTHER TREK SHOW?

Interestingly, in this 1991 interview he was asked whether he'd like to make a guest appearance on THE NEXT GENERATION. But because he'd seen how DeForest Kelley had looked under makeup applied to advance his appearance to age 137, Doohan wasn't too crazy about following in those venerable footsteps. "No, I just don't want to look that old. I was tremendously surprised that Leonard got on. I just don't see myself on there. But if somebody creates a situation—I don't bother to go and get scripts written for myself." And of course it was one year after Leonard Nimoy appeared on THE NEXT GENERATION that James Doohan reprised his role of Scotty (in a story which did not involve him having advanced one year in age) in the highly rated sixth season episode "Relics."

THE HELMSMAN

George Takei   © 1988 Smeal/Ron Galella Ltd.

CHAPTER 16

HIKARU SULU, HELMSMAN

Hawaii was the birthplace of Hikaru Sulu. His parents, Isao and Mitsuko Sulu, who were both of Japanese heritage, were a botanist and a poet. The family moved to agricultural station Wexler VIII early in Hikaru's life, so the boy saw little of his lush, tropical birthplace back on Earth, and in fact was so young when he left that he remembered it only from his parents descriptions.

While his mother, an agricultural specialist, researched practical concerns, Hikaru's father had become one of the better known poets of the Federation, writing frequently about Wexler VIII, a planet of extreme contrasts. Because of the planet's position near two stars, and its tilt on its axis, half of the world was lush like Earth, while the other half of the planet was a barren waste with the inhabitants living under envirodomes. All of Wexler VII, however, was almost completely devoid of sentient life. But Hikaru's father Isao found this a peaceful setting, one which was particularly conducive to creativity. It was a great place to get away from it all.

Hikaru attended a Federation colony school on Wexler. There he met children from the far flung worlds of the Federation. But even though the boy was fascinated by the stories of the other worlds his classmates had come from or visited, he longed to see the homeworld he had left when just an infant.

Since they had originally relocated due to his mother's work, it was the completion this stage of her work which signaled their next big move. So at the age of nine Hikaru and his family left the Wexler colony so that Mitsuko could begin thin-atmosphere tests of her research studies to determine the agricultural benefits. During the five years they spent going from planet to planet, Hikaru came to understand what the vastness of space truly held.

NOMADIC LIFE

Hikaru's education was constantly being interrupted by his parents' travels as they seldom remained on one world long enough for the boy to complete a full year of schooling there. Needless to say, establishing lasting friendships was next to impossible. Spending so much time around his mother and her peers, without kids his own age to be with, Hikaru eventually took an interest in his mother's work. Hikaru became very interested in plants and how they functioned. Photosynthesis fascinated him. In spite of an adult career which would take him in directions of command and control of a starship, the botany which formed the basis of his mother's career remained his lifelong avocation.

Being constantly on the move, Hikaru found that one of the few constants he could depend on were books. In particular he found himself entranced by classic adventure stories, such as those of Robin Hood, the Three Musketeers, and Medieval Europe in general. Although not directly related to his interest in reading swashbucklers (well, perhaps a little related), Hikaru eventually picked up fencing as a physical diversion in the confined spaces of an envirodome. Usually, Hikaru fenced against automated programmed drones, but when he

was lucky, he would run into another fencing enthusiast. Hikaru loved the challenge of personal competition, especially when it was against a real opponent rather than a drone. It was then his mind and spirit against another in a challenge which involved more than just reflexes.

But as time passed and he grew older, life inside envirodomes on thin-atmosphere planets began to grow confining for him. He had no friends his own age and he began to grow restless as his old loves of reading and fencing were no longer enough by themselves. He needed something more. Hikaru discovered that he gained a peculiar thrill from piloting the station's hovercraft. Here he was in charge, and although he couldn't go far with it outside the dome, the sensation of being at the controls of the craft awakened something in him.

AT HOME IN THE STARS

Hikaru's use of the hovercraft was strictly unauthorized, but because of how important it was to be able to experience these unique thrills, he was always careful not to abuse the craft and therefore never was caught by the station authorities.

His family returned to Wexler once again when Hikaru was fifteen. The boy had casually suggested that Earth might be a good place for his mother's experiments, but his parents preferred these worlds further out in the galactic rim. Mitsuko began working on other projects which did not require the frequent relocations Hikaru had experience all of his life up until then.

But now Hikaru was having trouble keeping up in his new classes on Wexler. Each time the Sulus had moved to another planet, Hikaru's curriculum had changed at least slightly, and the boy had never been in any one place long enough to complete the work he had begun there. Isao Sulu tutored his son to try to help him catch up and fill in the wholes in his education, but Hikaru was still uncertain when it came to academics, especially pure mathematics.

A WORLD APART

Hikaru gave more serious thought to his boyhood dreams of going to Japan as his graduation from high school drew near. He wanted to explore the culture of his heritage first-hand. The youth planned to study at the University of Tokyo to get a degree in botany and agriculture. Eventually Hikaru hoped to start a small experimental hydrofarm on one of the islands of the Japanese archipelago.

But before he could return to Earth, Hikaru had to relearn the language he had been born into. His parents supported their son's decision and Isao offered to tutor Hikaru in spoken and written Japanese. Soon the day came when the boy was ready to return to his ancestral home.

Upon arriving at the vast spaceport in Tokyo, Hikaru absorbed the sights of the city which spread out before him, and reveled in an ecstasy of personal triumph. To him it was like finally reaching the Emerald City of Oz, but in making that comparison he should have remembered that Oz was not all that it promised to be.

Hikaru arrived at the his dorm room at the university where he met his roommate. He introduced himself in perfect Japanese, whereupon the other laughed and remarked, "You speak like my grandfather." That was Hikaru's first shock. The culture he had long studied and admired was in many ways now a thing of the past, existing only in books.

SWASH-BUCKLER

Hikaru found that in spite of all his training, and perhaps even because of it, he could not fit in with his modern Japanese surroundings. "When I went to Earth, I had visions of medievalism, samurai tradition, a place where I could step into a role and be accepted unconditionally. Instead of mountains and rolling hills, I saw a technopolis. I found out that, like on any of the other worlds I had visited, I still had to prove myself. In some ways it was really worse. In the six months I ended up staying there, I found it no better or worse than any other planet," said Sulu of his first return to Earth since childhood.

Disillusioned and disheartened by these experiences, Sulu began searching for something else he could call home. Throughout his life he had traveled so much that there was no world he felt truly at home at. It was as though the stars themselves were his home. It was thoughts like these that attracted him to the possibilities inherent in Starfleet. That and his memories of being at the helm of the hovercraft.

Hikaru's next project was getting into Starfleet Academy. Wanting to attend and actually getting in were two very different things. He learned of the procedures and took the required achievement and aptitude tests. Much to his surprise, he found that while his achievement in applied mathematics was barely average, his aptitude was off the charts. His problem had not been that he wasn't good at math, merely that his schooling in it had been deficient due to his frequent moves and the interruptions of his studies.

Sulu decided to apply his interest in botany as a starting point in Starfleet and majored in that field. Starfleet required people who were well rounded in many areas, not just specialized in one to the exclusion of all others. Looking for something to occupy his down time, Sulu found that Starfleet Academy had a fencing society. Working with them he was able to further develop his skills, and build a powerful physique as well. Through enthusiasm and natural swashbuckling charm, Sulu easily acquired friends and acquaintances.

Hikaru found that he was a natural teacher who could explain things to others easily. Here people appreciated his talents and didn't mock his interests or his ways. He had finally found somewhere he could fit in. His tutoring abilities turned him into something of a "jack of all trades." In return for his help with some of the more mundane realities of Academy life, people showed Hikaru the more exciting things in life. One day, in return for emergency biochemistry lessons, a friend got Sulu onto the Academy helm trainers. Hikaru found himself fascinated by this and experimented with the Academy's helm simulators, playing the same games he played with the ag-station's hovercraft in his teen years. That old feeling was coming back.

NAVIGATION

While Hikaru broke all sorts of simulator records, he still needed to improve his actual math skills to take advantage of what he was discovering about himself. Turning to one of his friends, an engineering major named T'Skala, she tutored him in helm and navigation design. With her help, Sulu learned. T'Skala also showed his simulator tapes to her instructors, who recognized genuine talent when they saw it. A professor quickly contacted Sulu and offered to change his field of study. Sulu transferred his major to helm/navigation.

After spending a childhood bouncing from one planet to the next with no control over his destination, piloting finally gave him a feeling of control over his life. He found that piloting ships brought real-life applicability to the mathematics he had difficulty with in high school. His parents finally journeyed back to Earth to see their son graduate from the Academy and watch him board the USS Artemis for his cadet cruise. The Artemis was a small scout ship which made runs between the Sol system and Alpha Centauri. As an assistant helm officer, Sulu enjoyed piloting the spacecraft because of her small size. She responded quickly and sensitively under his deft control. This had hovercrafts beat hands down.

DEEP SPACE SKILLS

Hikaru was a full commissioned ensign when he returned to Earth after spending a year in space. Then he entered Starfleet Academy School, Starfleet's "grad school" for those officers who wanted to gain their own commands. Sulu spent a year in classroom sessions, more simulators and finally the notorious Kobayashi Maru no-win scenario. In the simulation, the Klingons destroyed Sulu's ship piece by piece. When he realized his hopeless situation, he ordered his crew away in the life-pods, staying himself. He took the helm of the dying ship, and worked the same magic he did in the simulators, maniacally bent on trying to take as many Klingon warships as he could with him as an honor guard. Sulu did a respectable job. By the time his vessel blew into a million pieces, he had destroyed six Klingon cruisers, earning the all-time record.

Sulu racked up a distinguished record at the Academy and graduated with a promotion to lieutenant, junior grade. Hikaru was posted to the destroyer Xerxes as a full helmsman. When Sulu returned to deep space, he found that while many of his comrades were awestruck by this experience, Sulu felt reassured and comfortable. To him the stars were his home.

CAPTAIN SULU

Sulu returned with the Xerxes after a three year mission in previously unexplored space. His commander on the Xerxes saw something special in the young helmsman and knew the new heavy cruisers would benefit by Sulu's superb piloting skill. The next one to be launched, the Enterprise, would need a helmsman of Sulu's talent, youthful tenacity, and enthusiasm.

These same qualities led to Sulu being promoted to command of his own starship years later, following the completion by the Enterprise of its five year mission and its redeployment to space fol-

lowing the vessel's replacement and rechristening. Lt. Sulu became Commander Sulu of the starship Excelsior. As Captain of the Excelsior fate stepped in when Sulu saved his old starship, the Enterprise, from a Klingon attack. Now it was time for Sulu to make his own legends, just as Captain Kirk had done.

CHAPTER 17

MORE THAN A HELMSMAN: GEORGE TAKEI

Born in the Boyle Heights district of Los Angeles, George lived there peacefully with his family until World War Two. Then the lives of many people across the world were disrupted by that great global conflict, including that of many Japanese Americans living on the West Coast of the United States. The attack on Pearl Harbor made America fear for the safety of its borders, and in California in particular there was a perceived danger of a Japanese invasion of the U.S. mainland. When the President of the United States signed an executive order authorizing the relocation of Japanese Americans away from the west coast (due to a perceived internal espionage threat) George and his family were forcibly relocated to a detention camp in Arkansas. From there they were moved again to another U.S. internment camp at Tule Lake in Northern California. Although George now resents what was done, he was too young at the time it happened to really understand what was going since in 1942-45 he was just a small child.

Originally George was fascinated with architectural design and he began his college education as an architecture student at the University of California at Berkeley. Later he transferred to the Los Angeles Campus of the university. There George majored in Theatre Arts, with a minor in Latin American Studies. He graduated in 1960 with a Bachelor of Arts degree.

Takei made his professional debut in a PLAYHOUSE 90 production during the time he was attending U.C.L.A. Concurrent with his university studies, George furthered his training as an actor at the Desilu Workshop, a studio he would have a lot of contact with in just a couple more years.

TAKEI'S TRAVELS

In 1963, George made another leap forward on the scale of experience. After living in New York City for several months, trying to break into professional acting, he left for Europe. During his travels across the European continent by bicycle, hitch-hiking and second-class trains, he sandwiched in attendance at the Shakespeare Institute at Stratford-on-Avon. Takei's wanderlust has also taken him on camping expeditions into the rugged Rocky Mountains, as well as a foray into the Alaskan panhandle, and numerous trips into Baja California.

Upon returning from Europe to Hollywood, George found that he had to work hard to find acting work, but finally he began to achieve some success. During that time, George racked up credits on such TV shows as PERRY MASON, HAWAIIAN EYE, THE ISLANDERS, ALCOA PREMIERE, CHECKMATE, MR. NOVAK, THE WACKIEST SHIP IN THE ARMY, I-SPY, THE JOHN FORSYTHE SHOW, BOB HOPE CHRYSLER THEATRE, BRACKEN'S WORLD, FELONY SQUAD, IRONSIDE, IT TAKES A THIEF, MR. ROBERTS, MY THREE SONS, VOYAGE TO THE BOTTOM OF THE SEA, THE TWILIGHT ZONE and many more.

George's TWILIGHT ZONE episode, "The Encounter," is no longer broadcast as part of the regular syndication package and in fact has not been seen on American television in decades. It originally aired May 1st, 1964 and deals with Neville Brand, as a middle-aged World War Two vet, who has a samurai sword in his attic which he took from the body of a surrendering Japanese soldier he'd brutally killed at the end of the war. Takei is a young man whose father was a traitor who signaled the Japanese planes into their targets at Pearl Harbor. When Takei picks up the sword he first becomes possessed by the spirit of the solider who had been murdered, but he soon comes to his senses. The Neville Brand character, a hateful bigot, has nothing left to live for any more and wants the young Japanese man to kill him. He refuses, but Brand gets in a scuffle, falls on the sword and dies. Knowing he'll be blamed, the young Japanese man grabs the sword and leaps from an attic window to his death.

In reality there is no recorded case of any Japanese American traitors in World War Two. The suggestion that there was, even in this fictional context, doubtlessly inspired complaints. The episode was subsequently pulled and has not been aired since the '60s, although bootleg copies exist in the great home video underground.

George Takei was cast on STAR TREK beginning with the second pilot, "Where No Man Has Gone Before." In that episode he's described as being a botanist. But once the series went into production he became a helmsman, apparently to make him a part of the highly visible bridge crew. A botanist, after all, wouldn't appear on the bridge very often nor would he figure in many storylines. In spite of how little Takei really had to do in many episodes, he was still a highly visible presence in the series. A few episodes, most notably "Shore Leave," "The Naked Time" and "Mirror, Mirror" did spotlight the actor to particularly good effect. The fact that those are 3 of the best episodes in the entire series makes his presence on the show as a whole even more memorable.

During the first season of STAR TREK, George managed to work in an appearance on MISSION: IMPOSSIBLE since his limited screen time allowed him days off from the show. During year two George had to request additional time off when he had the chance to appear in the feature film THE GREEN BERETS starring John Wayne. Because of Takei's absence, a new addition to the STAR TREK cast, Walter Koenig, found his position strengthened as he was given a few extra scenes to take up the slack left by Takei for those few weeks George was absent.

George Takei's motion picture credits include A MAJORITY OF ONE, RED LINE 7000, HELL TO ETERNITY, AN AMERICAN DREAM, WALK DON'T RUN, NEVER SO FEW, JOSIE'S CASTLE, THE LOUDMOUTH, THE YOUNG DIVORCEES PT 109 and WHICH WAY TO THE FRONT. After STAR TREK, George appeared on episodes of such TV series as KUNG FU, THE SIX MILLION DOLLAR MAN, BAA BAA BLACK SHEEP, CHICO AND THE MAN, HAWAII FIVE-O and MIAMI VICE.

LIFE ON THE BIG SCREEN

Takei's feature film debut was in the movie ICE PALACE, in which he co-starred with Richard Burton. George played a character who was seen over many years of his life, which required old age makeup not unlike what was used in the STAR TREK episode "The Deadly Years." Unfortunately, George's role in the film is a bit unsettling to watch as Takei plays a stereotyped Japanese houseboy. It's incredible to be watching it and to suddenly realize that it's George Takei because the characterization is rather extreme and the actor almost unrecognizable.

What makes it tolerable is that seeing it becomes somewhat like watching someone you know doing an outrageous imitation. It's meant to be funny, although in actuality the characterization is rather demeaning as no one would portray a character in such a manner in films today lest it be dubbed Japan-bashing. Although the film was made at a time when such characterizations were common (including having the Japanese characters played by Occidental actors wearing exaggerated make-up, such as Mickey Rooney in BREAKFAST AT TIFFANYS), it is a bit embarrassing when viewed today.

George's interests outside of acting include involving himself in political causes. George was a California representative at the 1972 Democratic National Convention, and in the fall of 1973 he ran unsuccessfully for Mayor Bradley's vacated council seat in Los Angeles. Takei competed against twenty-two other candidates, and it became such a rough campaign that the local television station had to stop showing STAR TREK reruns which featured George in them because the other candidates were threatening to demand equal time. When the final ballots were cast, George came in second. Actually he was one of the only two candidates who were considered to be serious contenders by the voters and by the media.

George has appeared in all six STAR TREK motion pictures and was particularly happy with THE UNDISCOVERED COUNTRY because he was made captain of his own starship. He isn't exaggerating when he urges Paramount to create a new STAR TREK spin-off and call it "CAPTAIN SULU." In the seventies, between the cancellation of STAR TREK and the revival of the series as motion pictures, Takei continued to make occasional television appearances, including a dual role on an episode of HAWAII FIVE-O. Takei also recreated the voice of his character of Lt. Sulu on the STAR TREK animated series produced in 1974-75.

Also in 1975 George starred in a PBS production of the play "Year of the Dragon" on THEATRE IN AMERICA. In this dramatic production, Takei played a bitter Japanese American who hates his life and the fact that he has to act as a tourist guide in L.A.'s "Little Tokyo." His character in some respects is a parody of his role in ICE PALACE as he finds himself having to pretend to act like such a stereotype for the hated tourists, but at home, behind-closed-doors, all he can do is talk about how much he hates the people he must depend on to make a living because of what they think of him and how they look down on him because of his ancestry. It is a powerful performance that can only startle people who are used to seeing him as Sulu and the narrow characterization he has been given on STAR TREK.

In the eighties, Takei played a drug lord on an episode of MIAMI VICE. George also hosted an informational TV series titled EXPRESSION EAST/WEST which dealt with issues involving human relationships. With author Robert Asprin, George co-wrote the science fiction novel MIRROR FRIEND, MIRROR FOE for the short-lived Playboy Press. A sequel has been discussed for many years but to date it has not been written.

He has recently appeared in a two motion pictures in major roles. One is RETURN FROM THE RIVER KWAI and the other is PRISONERS OF THE SUN. For the latter George received particularly good reviews in his role of a World War Two commandant of a prisoner of war camp who is put on trial for committing war crimes. Again, a powerful performance from an actor who is all too seldom given the opportunity to show what he can do. RETURN FROM THE RIVER KWAI encountered some controversy and may have been retitled because the owners of the motion picture BRIDGE ON THE RIVER KWAI considered the title a copyright infringement even though there really is a river Kwai in southeast Asia.

As to what George will be doing in the future of STAR TREK, he's open to any exciting offers.

CHAPTER 18

CAPTAINING HIS OWN SHIP

STAR TREK VI: THE UNDISCOVERED COUNTRY ushered in a new chapter in the life of Lt. Sulu, who was promoted to Commander Sulu. Now that Sulu has his own ship, he's actually no longer a part of the crew of the Enterprise. But does that bother him?

"You think I'm sad and lonely out there by myself without my friends?" Takei said, laughing uproariously. Clearly Sulu's position alone opens up an avenue for another possible sequel. "Maybe I need to recite the history of the STAR TREK movies. The very first film was titled THE MOTION PICTURE, suggesting that that's it. That's the movie. That was released and did megabusiness. And so they started talking about the only sequel because sequels generally do about 80% of the business of the preceding one. They didn't think STAR TREK would do that, but nevertheless it stands to make some money.

"But number two was supposed to be the last one—so final that we killed off Spock, and you can't imagine STAR TREK continuing without Spock. That was released. It did megabusiness. So then they started talking about a trilogy. That was kind of trendy at that time. But that means three, because it wouldn't be a trilogy if they did more. Number three was supposed to be the very last one. The Enterprise went down in flames and that was the real end because that was the real star. You can't have STAR TREK without the Enterprise. That made two tons of money.

"Then you started hearing about the last STAR TREK. The final one—number four, and now we've done six and that's what they're telling you again. The last one! Stick around until late January [1992] when the box office figures are in. Then you'll start hearing about the ultimate STAR TREK," he said, laughing. But while the box office for STAR TREK VI was very good, certainly superior to STAR TREK V, it didn't crack a hundred million in the United States the way STAR TREK IV—THE VOYAGE HOME did. So no new voyages of the original crew have yet been scheduled after all, in spite of George Takei's optimistic predictions, based as they were on the start and stop history of the motion pictures since 1979.

"And let me also cite something else. The denouement scene at the end on the bridge where the captain of the Enterprise, the torn and tattered Enterprise thanks the captain of that majestic craft, the starship Excelsior. And then he roars off into the galaxy. And McCoy says, 'By God that's a big ship.' And then Scotty chimes in with, 'Aye, but not so big as her captain, I think.' Now I think that's a pretty wide open end!"

Still and all, Leonard Nimoy did flatly state that STAR TREK VI was the last one.

"Leonard is not the final word," George pointed out. "Even the top executive is not the final word. You know who has the final word? The audience." But using that logic, shouldn't STAR TREK V have been the last one? George thought that was a pretty funny observation. "Oh! That wound that was healing! It's starting to get wet again! That's a cruel cut! STAR TREK V was, as we euphemistically put it, a disappointment. But what really gave birth to STAR TREK VI was that some of the marketing people discovered that 1991 happened to be the silver anniversary of STAR TREK. What a great opportunity to market t-shirts, medallions, stamps, underpants—all sorts of things can be sold. Except you need a vehi-

cle. You need another movie, and so that's what saved us despite the disappointment of number five."

INSIDE SULU

How much of George Takei is in Mr. Sulu?

"It's a character created by Gene Roddenberry. I was cast in it so inevitably there is a little bit of my persona, my idiosyncrasies that bleed through. But I must say that it's Gene Roddenberry's vision and imagination that gave the specifics to my character. Sulu is an avid collector. He's a good professional first of all, but he has a lot of idiosyncrasies and I wish that we could have explored some of that aspect of Sulu a bit more—both in the film and TV versions. But I would say it's a combination of Gene Roddenberry's imagination and some of my own personality traits that I brought with me."

Since Sulu remained a minor character during the run of the television series, had he ever hoped for an episode which might have spotlighted his character a bit more?

"Oh, it was awfully frustrating. I kept peppering Gene Roddenberry during the TV series and Harve Bennett during the movie series with ideas, with plot possibilities, and character qualities that could explore a good deal more of this fascinating character. It's very difficult. I think the character is interesting enough so that we can see more of Sulu. Not just getting the focus on an episode of the television series, but I've been actively lobbying Paramount to come back with a weekly series, regular television version of STAR TREK, our generation under the title CAPTION SULU." He laughs at that, knowing how self-aggrandizing it sounds. "I think that's going to be a sure fire ratings grabber."

GENE'S FINAL DAYS

Less than two months before the release of STAR TREK VI, Gene Roddenberry died, a fact which couldn't help but bring a note of sadness to the 25th anniversary year of the series.

"This is Gene's vision. It's his creation. We are his children. He left us a great legacy and his absence is definitely going to be felt. But another part of the legacy that he left us; he was aware of his mortality. As a matter of fact his passing was not unexpected. It was a jolt and it was very painful to see this vigorous, dynamic man reduced by small hits. He had a series of strokes. His speech slurred and was at one time confined to a wheelchair. He needed a cane and his male nurse

assisting him to the point where he could walk. But it wasn't that strong policeman's stride, it was this old man's shuffle. It was painful to see that.

"But Gene made sure that what he had given birth to would continue on, and with THE NEXT GENERATION he had people that shared that vision and had talent and the kind of integrity and strength that kept that vision intact. And certainly with the STAR TREK movies his participation was as an executive consultant, and the real active creators were people that he had charged with carrying on the flame, so to speak.

I think his vision is intact. Two days before he passed on he saw the final cut of STAR TREK VI and he was very, very happy. That was another pat on the back that he gave us before he passed on. So his vision and his legacy will continue because he's left us, as part of that legacy, people that share his talent and philosophy and what STAR TREK is all about."

ABOARD THE EXCELSIOR

One of Sulu's crewmen on the Excelsior in STAR TREK VI is actor Christian Slater. "I have a new puppy," George added, seemingly going off in another direction but tying it quickly back to

Christian Slater. "It's the cutest thing and it just wiggles and the tail wags and it bounces up and down. Well, that was Christian Slater. He did everything he could to lobby to get to be on the set just to wear that uniform. He was a fan from the time he was a child. That was his big dream.

My childhood dream was to swashbuckle in Sherwood Forest. He did that but his dream was to wear the Starfleet uniform, and he was literally like my puppy, bouncing up and down, wiggling and saying, 'Look at this! This spot comes down and then it can go up again and you can tear it right down,' and he goes dashing down the corridor to climb up the ladder and say, This is where Scotty did such and such, and he'd be waving at us. He was literally a 21 year old kid in his fantasy land."

But George can well understand how it feels for someone to meet their personal heroes. "A few months ago, Nichelle Nichols and Jimmy Doohan and I got a special visit to the Kennedy Space Center at Cape Canaveral. I've always seen the people in our space program as our real heroes. The people who really are working on the frontiers of our time and doing it in fact. And I particularly recall meeting the Japanese-American astronaut before the Challenger tragedy. And I remember the pride I felt in these men and women out there doing what we did fictionally.

"When Nichelle and Jimmy and I visited there, I went there somewhat in awe of what they're doing. We worked on a set but there they are doing what they're doing in reality, facing the real challenges. And yet they came up to us and told us that they went into the space program because of us. They were inspired to study aeronautics or astronautics or this area of technology because as kids they watched STAR TREK and they were inspired. So there's that both humbling and flattering symbiosis. People that I consider my real heroes were inspired by us in our fictional capacity and there they are, really in fact blazing that frontier for us."

Since George Takei has been closely identified with STAR TREK for 25 years, he's certainly experienced many of the benefits that come with that sort of celebrity, but what about the drawbacks?

"I know that some of my colleagues have complained about being imprisoned by their association with the characters that they played, and one would think that might be true for me as well. Interestingly enough it's been an asset. The other thing that might be considered a liability for an actor is that I'm a specific ethnic casting type, but both those things have been, ironically, assets to me because if you're associated with a show this popular and this long-lived and it's known by so many people, your name gets a certain currency.

"Earlier this year I had a film I did in Australia with Bryan Brown called PRISONERS OF THE SUN. All the other Japanese roles were cast out of Tokyo. The character that I was cast in was a Japanese aristocrat. Now I'm a third generation Japanese American, middle class, so that was an acting challenge, an acting reach for me, particularly because I'm working with Japanese from Japan of that culture. I'm confident enough in my talent, but I couldn't use my own personal experiential tools. The producer said to me they were looking at an international market and they found competent actors in Japan, but they couldn't find the combination of the competent actor who also could handle the English dialogue, who also was able to sell tickets in Japan as well as North America, South America and Europe. STAR TREK gave me that currency.

INSIDE TREK

What continues to make STAR TREK so special after 25 years?

"Well, it's a combination of a lot of things. On the surface it's good action/adventure. But beyond that it's really imaginative science fiction. It also provided a forum for those that were interested in social and political and environmental issues. It also comes down to just good luck. Being in the right place at the right time, chance and good fortune. All those things came into play in just the right combination."

At the time STAR TREK V was released to mixed reviews and much lower than expected ticket sales, some felt that the existence of the new weekly STAR TREK: THE NEXT GENERATION diverted interest away from the motion picture. But George Takei didn't feel that this really had anything to do with the problems the movie encountered.

"No, I think primarily it's the fact that STAR TREK V wasn't a good film," George candidly observed. "THE NEXT GENERATION is enjoying its popularity and it has its audience. Frankly I'm delighted that what STAR TREK stood for, the ideals and values, are transferable to a whole new group of actors with their own unique chemistry, and that they can take that and be as effective in communicating that as we've been."

UNRAVELING

Regarding STAR TREK V, George stated that he did feel that the movie was a disappointment.

"It is because you always do a film hoping for the best, and we also began the film hoping to do a good film and it isn't the film that it should've been. So maybe it's getting the business that it deserves. As Shakespeare said: 'The fault, dear Brutus, is not in our stars, but in ourselves.'

"They had four or five plots trying to work itself into a single thread. I would've selected just one of them and built a tight, gripping, riveting drama around that. There was a story about this messianic, driven individual who turns out to be Spock's half-brother. A confrontation between that individual and the Enterprise crew would have been an interesting piece of drama."

And then there was the story of the hostage-taking which was dealt with briefly.

"We were taken hostage and that is a very current issue today—the moral dilemma. Do we, in order to save a few people, jeopardize the entire society? It's an intriguing concept that lends itself to both science fiction and a gripping type of drama. I think that might have been the basis for a very interesting story.

"There was the possibility of another story. A planet that began with great optimism, hope and spirit; great promise, and it turns into this desert wasteland with desperate people scratching out an existence, vulnerable to any messiah who comes. I think that could have been developed into a fascinating story. It had a Lawrence of Arabia feel about it, but nothing happened with that."

And the film also had yet another parallel storyline involving the Klingons.

"Without any kind of explanation. Without any attempt to examine the relationship with the Klingons, we find them coming to Kirk's rescue at the very end. The Greeks had a term for an artificial ending for a play. They had God coming down in a machine to right all the complications that had been developed up to that point. They called it deus ex machina—God comes down on a machine. Well, I call the ending we had in STAR TREK V—Klingon ex machina—Klingon coming out of a clear blue sky to resolve the drama.

"So all those things, all those plots, had interesting possibilities in themselves, but when they came together and they tried to be worked together in the messy way that it was, then you just don't hold an audience. I think that was the primary reason for the failure of STAR TREK V."

RECASTING

Since George is so identified with the role of Sulu, could anyone else ever play that role instead of him?

"Paramount seriously considered that for a time a couple of years ago, right after STAR TREK V, because the notion of doing a movie for the

25th anniversary came up. They considered a lot of factors and this notion was suggested of doing a prequel where we have all of the original characters, but played by younger actors who resemble us. Now this movie, to celebrate the silver anniversary, 25 years, with brand new faces—what a stupid idea! And yet that idea got some momentum and so here again I dutifully reported to my bosses last year. I did twelve conventions in a row, three months, every weekend I did STAR TREK conventions, and I told them, you write to Frank Mancuso, [at Paramount] who is your underling.

"I've been involved in this arena from way back. I campaigned for George McGovern. And the bosses gave the marching order to the hired hand, Frank Mancuso, and he got the message. I mean the message was of tidal wave proportions."

Could it have been that the person at Paramount who suggested this idea felt that it was embarrassing to feature a cast of older performers, whose ages range from 50 to 70, as heroes in an action oriented film? Hollywood tends to resist the idea of having older people as heroic figures, unless there's a singular aspect to them, like Sean Connery, who's a profound exception to the rule. But STAR TREK flies in the face of that Hollywood tradition.

"The very fact that STAR TREK's lasted 25 years is flying in the face of tradition in Hollywood, and I think that's one of the attractive things about STAR TREK today. We live in a very transient and temporary world. Political policy is made in two year increments. Business plans are based on the next quarterly report. Everything is short term. Even marriages don't last. And here we have a group of people that audiences have grown up with for twenty-five years. There's something very comforting. Something very stable. There's something that they can rely on with that longevity itself," Takei stated.

TREK MATURES

"Sure, some of us have changed. Some have become big actors. I think that's part of it, because the people that have grown with us have grown with us and it's reflecting their lives as well. Now they're bringing their children, who are teenagers. Our fandom is growing, not just because we're getting more advocates but they're also propagating."

Which brings us to sex in STAR TREK. Why hasn't there been more sex in STAR TREK?

"Have you ever watched the TV series?! Kirk was promiscuous with every alien life form!" he said, laughing. "Who knows, we might have STAR TREK X: GERIATRIC SEX or something like that. To boldly go where we haven't been before! In STAR TREK VI there's a very interesting alien relationship between Spock and Valeris. You say sex but you think in terms of humanoid relationships. Now we're talking about Vulcans and Valeris is pure Vulcan. Spock is half human. So how are we to judge what's going on with them? And there was that one alien creature that Kirk had that fight with. He kicked the creature in the knees and it responded the way it did. So how do you know whether we're being very sexy or not? You know the mind-meld could be the most passionate, the most pornographic of activities!"

AN ACTIVE CAREER

James Doohan stated that STAR TREK definitely typecast him, but George doesn't feel that his career has been impacted in that way at all.

"I've had a lot of interesting guest shots to do on television and they've been quite varied. None of them has been a very efficient helmsman of a starship. One was a rather eccentric janitor who's a collector of celebrity trash. I did another one on MIAMI VICE where I played an international banker who was thoroughly corrupt. There has been a good, interesting, spicy variety to the kinds of roles that I've been able to play.

"In my case, my association with STAR TREK has been a real asset; a bonus. It's given currency to the name George Takei and many producers have said that they cast me because they know I'll be bringing along an audience with me. The STAR TREK audience will follow me to see PRISONERS OF THE SUN or RETURN FROM THE RIVER KWAI or MURDER, SHE WROTE."

[This chapter also includes material culled from a second interview with George Takei conducted by Michael Ruff in November 1989.]

Walter Koenig   © 1993 Ron Galella Ltd.

CHAPTER 19

NAVIGATOR PAVEL CHEKOV

The Russian city of Leningrad was the birthplace of Pavel Chekov. He was the only child of Ivan, the city manager, and his wife, Paulina. Ivan saw to it that his son had the finest schooling, and he gave the boy a love of his heritage by telling his son about the heroes of mother Russia. But Ivan's love of his country was so great that he believed it was the jewel of the planet, and that Earth was built on the discoveries and the creations of Russian culture and technology.

In school, more was expected of the son of the city manager than of other boys. Pavel was the son of a man who had nothing in his youth but who had yet achieved power through personal perseverance. Ivan was a popular leader, who worked hard for what he got, and Pavel was expected to achieve twice what his father did. Even Pavel's friends were the "gifted children" of whom great things were expected.

Working for the future was the constant subject of discussion, even when Pavel went out with his friends after school. Pavel's mother, Paulina, saw the drawbacks in this and managed to convinced the men in her family to take vacations. But wherever they went, Paulina would end up relaxing while her husband made personal political contacts and her son studied the local history. Pavel adjusted his life to this intensity.

FIRST LOVE

If Pavel had a weakness, it was a certain young lady named Irina Galilulan. Both beautiful and intelligent, Pavel still was uncertain what to make of her. She was a rival and yet he liked her. When he was with her he didn't want to think about his studies; he wanted to think about her.

His parents soon recognized what was happening as Pavel talked about Irina constantly. The youth had never spoken of his other friends this way before. Pavel's mother recognized that her son was falling in love, even if he didn't understand it yet. Paulina had been an exchange student on Vulcan many years before, and while she respected their drive for success and their system of logic, she had married a human. It turned out he might as well have been a Vulcan but for pointed ears. She didn't want her son to fall into the same trap. Non-emotion was very good for Vulcans, but humans needed their emotions.

Initially Ivan disapproved of Pavel's growing interest in Irina. While he'd first dismissed it as just a teenage phase, it became clear as months passed that Irina was a vital part of young Pavel's life. Ivan tried to convince his son to be more like him; to find success first and then worry about falling in love. But Paulina knew that Pavel's emotions were not as tightly ordered as his father's.

CONFLICTING GOALS

Pavel found himself uncertain which route to follow. His mother approved of his romance with Irina while his father felt that the boy was becoming too serious too soon. To make matters worse, Irina was becoming less interested in her studies, which Pavel couldn't understand either. She often talked about living a different life, a freer life which concentrated much more on needs of the human spirit than on the needs of human society.

But Pavel was still self-possessed enough to understand that he had a duty to himself and his family. But he loved Irina and didn't want to lose her any more than he wanted to abandon the goals he'd been working towards for so long.

Irina tried to make Pavel understand her ideas and sometimes after school took him to a wilderness area a distance from the city. Pavel liked being alone with Irina as it made the woodlands they sat in seem even more vibrant and alive. Her presence made the very air shine. It was as though she was one with nature as she showed him how to build a shelter, which flora were edible; how to follow the creatures of nature in silence so as to see their total uninhibited beauty.

But soon the gentle trips gave way to something more insistent. Irina was Pavel to abandon his studies and run away with her, leave the city and all it represented far behind. To his surprise, Pavel found himself attracted to the idea. Don't worry about the future, just live in the here and now. But weren't his responsibilities also a part of the here and now?

Each night in the Chekov household, Ivan would bring home more opportunities to his son for his future if only his son remain diligent in his studies as he had been in the past. Pavel couldn't bear to let his father down and waste all of the opportunities his father had been working to get for him. He would soon have to make a decision, and in doing so Pavel knew that something important to him would be lost no matter what he decided to do.

ULTIMATUM

Irina wasn't willing to let Pavel decide on his own, and so she forced the issue with him. He would have to choose between what she wanted for them, or what his father had always taught him was the intelligent path to follow. Irina was going to leave to join some mysterious friends far from the city and she wanted Pavel to accompany her. Irina pleaded with Pavel to join her, spoke of beaches to walk on, children to share and life to enjoy together.

Pavel reminded her of her studies, the investment she, her parents, and society had made into her skills. He told her she had to do what was right and honor her parents—live up to society's expectations. She rejected that outright, saying her life was her own to live. Pavel told her of the grand opportunities that lie before them if only they persevered. She told him he was unfeeling; she wanted him to leave.

Heartbroken, Pavel returned home to his family. But the worst was yet to come. Irina was not in school the next day, nor the day after. Not even her parents knew where she had gone. Pavel would not see Irina again for many years. He searched for her frantically but no trace of where she had gone could be found. Irina had been there for so long, that now without her there was a hole in his life. But his father kept pushing him. After all, he still had his responsibilities, and his future. But now it was a future that Irina would never be a part of.

THE LURE OF STARFLEET

Pavel Chekov continued his studies and upon completing high school he entertained the offers from several universities. But for sensitive youth, Leningrad had grown stark, empty, bleak and hollow. He saw a future of more work, laboring towards some unresolved goal without Irina there to share it with him.

When Pavel received the invitation from Starfleet, it took him by surprise. His studies and his plans had always centered around Leningrad and his home. But what did Leningrad hold for him now? He thought it over for some time and decided to apply.

Paulina was concerned for her son's safety in Starfleet, but his father was supportive of Pavel's choice. But then Ivan didn't realize just how far away from Leningrad Pavel wanted to get. He expected his son's sojourn in Starfleet to be a respectable temporary steppingstone for the boy. Ivan himself had served honorably in the Merchant Marine for a brief time. It had taught good discipline. But Pavel was beginning to see Starfleet as not just a diversion or a side trip on his path to success, but perhaps the goal itself; the one he'd been working towards without really knowing where he was going.

Pavel had spent years working hard at his studies, and so the Starfleet entrance exams didn't overly challenge him. He scored high, but once Pavel was in the Academy attending classes, he found them to be just as rigorous as anything he'd been involved with before.

Pavel found that the attitude behind the hard work at the Academy was different from what he had known growing up. His father had always pushed discipline as "patriotism," and an obligation. In Starfleet, cadets accepted self-discipline because they craved it. The cadets felt purpose behind the hard work, and saw the goals they wanted to attain. Pavel Chekov came to respect this voluntary self-imposed rigor more than the forced control of his youth. To Pavel, giving of yourself because you wanted to meant more than obligatory sacrifice.

DATE WITH DESTINY

Pavel graduated from Starfleet Academy with the highest honors. He was soon assigned to the USS Hannibal, a destroyer, as his cadet cruise. Pavel worked on the Hannibal as the assistant navigator and often found that his duties relegated him to the "night" shift when ship's onboard activity was at a minimum. But this was no milk run as the Hannibal was frequently assigned to the Klingon border. The ship encountered the Klingons several times, engaging them in direct combat. The invaders were always repelled.

Chekov always kept his head in the most intense situations and proved time and again that he was a good crewman to have on hand under fire. The captain of the Hannibal began to take notice of this young crewman, of his readiness to serve and his level-headedness in battle while others around him were losing their head. The Hannibal's commander noted Pavel was more skilled at the navigation console than were many veterans. The skipper commended the young officer and promoted him to assistant chief navigator.

Pavel returned to Starfleet Academy after the year's cadet mission was over. There he chose to attend the year-long Command School, in which he again distinguished himself. Pavel performed exactingly and methodically during the entire Kobayashi Maru test; everything was done in safety and by the book. While Pavel and his ship went down at the hands of the computer-driven Klingon fleet, his decisiveness saved more of the lives of his crew than did most other cadets. Pavel dreamed of the day he could command a starship of his own.

Once he was promoted to the rank of Ensign, Pavel eagerly looked forward to the ship where he would undertake his first five year mission. That vessel was to be the Enterprise. Under the command of James T. Kirk, this vessel was already legendary due to the engagements it had fought under its previous commanders, Robert April and Christopher Pike. Kirk was looking for a bridge crew-

man with just the qualifications Chekov's record indicated that he had: skill, a cool head and efficiency.

Chekov would learn a lot under Kirk's command, and he would come to recognize that even in Starfleet one could find a family as they faced seemingly hopeless odds together and came out the other side because of their combined skills. It was during this five year mission that Pavel would encounter Irina again. She had joined the troupe of a wandering Guru named Sevrin who believed they knew the way to Eden. And Chekov would be there when Irina finally discovered that pace and tranquillity could never be found by running away in search of them.

Chekov's loyalty would being him back to the Enterprise years later even after serving aboard the Grissom. There was only one Enterprise, and it was an even more amazing place to be than Leningrad had ever been.

CHAPTER 20

STAYING THE COURSE: WALTER KOENIG

On September 4, 1936, Walter Koenig was born in Chicago, Illinois. It wasn't long, though, before his parents moved Walter and his brother to the Inwood area of Manhattan where he grew up and attended school. Walter became interested in theater when he was attending high school. He first appeared on stage, though, in Riverdale, New York at the Fieldston High School of the Ethical Culture. His stage debut was made playing the title role in a production of "Peer Gynt." Walter also appeared there in "The Devil's Disciple."

In his summers, Walter became involved with working in upstate New York at camps for underprivileged children. His contribution, which is still employed today, involved the introduction of a theatre program which was, in truth, a thinly disguised psychodrama for disturbed and overly aggressive youngsters. This program was later incorporated into the camp's parent settlement house in the city for use with adults with similar problems. Koenig was a high school student when he devised these psychodramas.

Along with his theatrical talents, Walter shared an equal interest in psychiatry. As a result his first two years at Grinell College in Iowa were in pre-med courses. During his school vacations, he performed in summer stock in Vermont. When his father died, Walter moved with his mother and his brother to California. He transferred his college credits to U.C.L.A. and graduated from there with a B.A. in psychology.

ACTOR'S LIFE

But even while he had been seriously pursuing his psychology degree at U.C.L.A., he had also studied theater and become good friends with his professor, Arthur Friedman. Deciding that he wanted to try a career other than psychology, in spite of holding a degree, Walter relocated to New York and enrolled at the Neighborhood Playhouse upon the recommendation of Prof. Friedman. To meet expenses during this period, he worked as a hospital orderly, earning $75 a month. He found this to be a vastly more fulfilling experience than the usual starving actor job of waiting on tables. Walter spent two years doing off-Broadway work, but finally decided to return to Los Angeles.

Once back in L.A. he found that he was able to land a variety of roles on quite a variety of television shows. His first TV role was on the show DAY IN COURT. But his range as an actor was so great that he soon was playing such characters as a Swedish businessman, an American grape-picker, an Arabian rock and roll singer and a French resistance fighter. His television credits include appearances on MR. NOVAK, THE GREAT ADVENTURE, GIDGET, JERRICO, THE LIEUTENANT, BEN CASEY, COMBAT, THE GREAT ADVENTURE, IRONSIDE, MANNIX, MEDICAL CENTER, THE MEN FROM SHILOH, THE UNTOUCHABLES, and I-SPY.

Koenig's most prominent television role in the sixties, outside of STAR TREK, was in a one-hour episode of ALFRED HITCHCOCK PRESENTS titled "Memo From Purgatory." This episode was written by Harlan Ellison, drawn from his experiences when he ran with a street gang for 6 weeks to get material for a book. Koenig played a gang leader who discovers what the writer has written about him, and he isn't flattered by what he reads. It's an excellent episode of the series and through it Koenig met Ellison, with whom he has been good friends ever since.

ENTER CHEKOV

In 1967, Koenig answered a casting call for a new character who would appear on STAR TREK. Walter had actually never seen a complete episode of the show although he had been on the set once before when he visited an acquaintance who was working at Paramount. When Koenig initially joined the show it was in the second season and was on a week-to-week basis. He felt this made him insecure in his performance since he knew he could be written out of the show at any time. As it was he got a boost because series regular George Takei had taken a ten-week leave of absence to work on the John Wayne movie THE GREEN BERETS. As a result Chekov was getting scenes which had been written for Sulu.

The first episode Koenig appeared in was "Who Mourns For Adonais," a tale about an alien who had been regarded as a god by the Greeks when he visited the Earth thousands of years before. Since Walter was supposed to be a character who appealed to teenagers, his hair was supposed to be longer, in the tradition of the Beatles. But while Walter's hair was growing out to its proper length naturally, he had to wear a wig, which is quite apparent in this particular episode.

Purely from a dramatic point of view, Koenig's best role on the series was in the episode "Mirror, Mirror." In that teleplay which he appears as the sly, ruthless alternate universe Chekov who nearly succeeds in assassinating Captain Kirk. When the third season rolled around, Walter was signed on as a regular, guaranteed work for the entire year. He enjoyed doing STAR TREK and liked the people he worked with, many of whom he has remained close friends with over the years. Occasionally, though, he has had less than salutory comments about William Shatner, whom he felt looked down on the supporting players. Koenig most recently made a comment to that effect in the July 24, 1993 issue of TV GUIDE.

During the third season of STAR TREK, Gene Roddenberry stepped down as line producer over a scheduling dispute with the network. As a result Fred Frieberger was brought in to produce the show. Koenig never felt that Frieberger understood STAR TREK or gave the series its proper due. Koenig was particularly frustrated by the way he was forced to play his character in "The Way To Eden." Even though Chekov had been created to appeal to the younger audience members, when characters his own age board the Enterprise in that episode, Chekov is forced to treat them like anything but his contemporaries. Instead of having Chekov lured into their cause, the young ensign acts contemptuous of everything the young people represent, particularly their idealism. Koenig did not find much of what happened during the third season particularly pleasant.

BEYOND STAR TREK

In 1969, after the cancellation of STAR TREK, Koenig moved on, although his career momentum had slowed. He did appear in occasional TV shows and films but concentrated more on teaching acting. He appeared on a COLUMBO (in which William Shatner was the killer of the week) and in the TV movie GOODBYE RAGGEDY ANN with Martin Sheen and Mia Farrow. He also appeared in the unsold pilot THE QUESTOR TAPES, which was created by Gene Roddenberry. When Harlan Ellison created the short-lived syndicated series THE STARLOST, Koenig appeared in two episodes as the villainous alien named Oro.

On stage Walter Koenig played three roles in the highly acclaimed theatre group production of "The Deputy": a Jewish refugee, a Nazi sergeant and a Catholic monk. He also played a Welsh psychopath in "Night Must Fall."

Walter has extended his talents into the area of writing as well. His television writing credits include an episode of LAND OF THE LOST ("The Stranger") and also the episode "The Infinite Vulcan" for the animated STAR TREK. When the animated STAR TREK series was put together, there wasn't room in the budget for Walter to do the voice of Chekov, so instead Roddenberry offered him the chance to write an episode, which he happily accepted.

Koenig has also written scripts for such TV series as CLASS OF '65, THE POWERS OF MATTHEW STARR and FAMILY. In the book field Walter wrote a behind-the-scenes log about his experiences making STAR TREK—THE MOTION PICTURE called CHEKOV'S ENTERPRISE. And in 1988 he had a science fiction novel published titled BUCK ALICE AND THE ACTOR ROBOT. When Koenig got back the rights to CHEKOV'S ENTERPRISE a few years later, he found a new publisher. A new edition of the book was released in 1992 in a handsome trade paperback which features a new introduction by Harlan Ellison. His latest writing work is a comic book series, RAVER, from Malibu comics, a California based company.

STAR TREK AND THE STAGE

In films Walter also appeared in the movie DEADLY HONEYMOON as well as in all six STAR TREK motion pictures. In the STAR TREK movies he had his most prominent roles in THE WRATH OF KHAN and THE VOYAGE HOME.

Other than STAR TREK, his most recent film appearance was a starring role in the science fiction movie MOONTRAP. Although it had only a very limited theatrical release, the film has proven to be very popular on cable and on home video. A sequel has been discussed but hasn't yet come together.

Koenig appeared in MOONTRAP with his wife, actress Judy Levitt. Walter's entire family has gotten into acting in one form or another including his son Andrew and daughter Danielle. Andrew even had a continuing role on a series when he played the character "Boner" on the sit-com GROWING PAINS. Meanwhile, Danielle appeared in two episodes of LIFE GOES ON and on the short-lived series THE FANEILLI BOYS.

In September, 1989, Walter and his wife, Judy, appeared on the Los Angeles radio show "Hour 25" doing a dramatic reading of an unproduced TWILIGHT ZONE script titled "Say Hello, Mr. Quigley." In recent years Walter has toured with Mark Lenard in the Bernard Sabbath play "The Boys of Autumn." The play is a dramatic look at the fictional characters of Tom Sawyer and Huckleberry Finn when they encounter one another as adults and gradually reveal certain dark secrets about their past.

These days Walter considers himself to be a writer as much as an actor and continues to work on various projects, including marketing a screenplay he recently completed, and which he discusses in his interview just a few pages away from here.

CHAPTER 21

TALKING WITH CHEKOV

Koenig didn't board the Enterprise until the second season of the original TV series, but he's been along for the ride ever since. Now that it appears the original crew has had their final big screen adventure, Walter is willing to bid adieu to what he regards as an enjoyable flight.

"I think this is the last voyage," Koenig stated when asked whether the original crew of the Enterprise would be seeing any further adventures aboard that famous starship. "When you talk to Jimmy and Nichelle you're going to get something that's more closely aligned with George [Takei's] feeling. "Maybe it's because I feel a certain satisfaction with the way this picture works and there is a sense of closure here. Certainly there are certain pragmatic aspects as to why this should be the last film. There are many people in the media who feel we have overstayed our welcome to begin with."

Walter readily admits he dislikes comments along those lines. "It really bothers me. I wish I could say that it doesn't bother me, but it really bothers me. It bothers me because that seems to be the springboard for every comment that comes after. It's one thing to reflect on the fact that we certainly have aged over the course of 25 years, and even since the last film. But to condemn the project or the performers as a consequence of that I think is very unfair. But I see that, again and again."

Clearly some alterations have been made in the characters, but nothing detrimental to the series in any way. "We no longer have Bill thrusting his tongue down some young lady's throat, because that wouldn't work. That's not as likely, except that there are people who are 60 years old in positions of power who do have pretty young things. But we have made that concession. We don't get involved in hand-to-hand fighting because that would be, perhaps, stretching credibility. But in terms of reflexes, in terms of functioning on a ship. In terms of ideas, I don't think that we should be condemned as a group and summarily dismissed as a consequence of the age bracket."

NEW CHALLENGES

When it's all said and done, Walter does accept that this should be the last voyage for this Enterprise crew. "Well, I don't want to hear that abuse any more, but I don't know whether that's number one or not. I think the studio feels they have an up and coming contender waiting in the wings with THE NEXT GENERATION. I think they have taken the stand that this is the last picture, not that that stand is irrevocable. But their thinking now isn't along those terms. It's 25 years, we've done a bang-up job. We've made a whole thing about this being the last voyage and let's leave it at that.

"And then there's a certain amount of wish fulfillment on my part. I'm ready to let go. I'm not fed up. I'm not over saturated with STAR TREK, I'm just ready to let go and see if there's anything else out there. I'd like to be hungry again because with that little apprehension, with that need comes hopefully some inspiration and some creativity. I've been a little complacent as a consequence. That doesn't mean that I haven't done anything in the last 25 years but STAR TREK, but there's something to be said for additional motivation to feed your family."

Koenig only saw the completed STAR TREK VI shortly before meeting the press, and this had a profound impact on his feelings about STAR TREK at that time and what he had to say about it.

"It would have been much more difficult for me to wax poetic about STAR TREK, but having seen this picture and feeling so positive about it, and I'm no longer under salary. I'm not a company man at this juncture. I want everybody to see this picture because I think it's neat and if that means sitting for three days and doing 60 interviews so that the word gets out, I'm happy to do it. I get a little tired, but I'm happy to do it."

FIRST ENCOUNTER

Walter Koenig didn't join the cast of STAR TREK until the second season of the TV series, but he was aware of the show prior to his being cast and he recalled when he first encountered the series.

"I was flipping channels and I saw the Styrofoam rocks and I thought, this looks really cheap. I never watched an episode. A friend of mine was the casting director, and I was there for some other reason at Paramount, and I visited the set. I sort of said ho-hum and I didn't think anymore of it. When I was called in it was to do one episode and possibly to be reinvited should they like what I did. But nobody believes it when they say it's going to be a recurring role. It usually means they don't want to pay you very much. So I took it with a grain of salt. When I kept being asked back it was only over a period of time that I began to realize that I was really going to be in the show. I wasn't under contract at all that season. The last year of the show they put me under contract. But I had no guarantee and I didn't know, going on from week to week, if I was going to be with it. I did 39 episodes in two seasons."

During the ten years between the cancellation of the television series and the arrival of STAR TREK: THE MOTION PICTURE, Walter appeared at a number of STAR TREK conventions. He doesn't feel it was because he was necessarily out there proselytizing for the show's return so much as it was because he was an invited, and paid, guest.

"I've always been one of the most skeptical about the possibility of STAR TREK resurrecting in any form. Every time we were supposed to start it, we didn't, and that just sort of reinforced the idea that it's never going to happen. I think those are the reasons why I don't think that it's going to happen again. It is not inconceivable that it could come back. If this picture did gross $100 million, and if the fan reaction was so strong beyond simply the box office to keep it going, and they haven't been in the past. I guess it is possible that the people at Paramount could reconsider. That maybe we're killing the [golden] goose. I don't know."

THE MAGIC OF TREK

Walter has been attending conventions since the seventies, but in spite of his many group encounters with STAR TREK fans, he doesn't have an easy answer to the question of what attracts people to the series.

"I'm not sure there is a simple answer to that. I think it has to do with the very durability of the show, the fact that we have been around for so long. We represent something very stable. I think the audience likes that feeling of stability. Marriages last far shorter than our show has. But we have remained constant. The seven members of this cast are still together. I think that is very comforting. Of course there are many other reasons as well.

"I think the show addressed topical issues; it has made socio-political statements that have been positive. It suggests that the future will be an affirmative future. And of course the stories have been intelligently written and dimensionally performed."

Does he think that perhaps the fans are going a bit overboard by having huge conventions devoted to STAR TREK?

"I certainly hope so!" he said, laughing. "As long as the fans are going overboard that makes our project viable and keeps us working, and that is certainly something that is very agreeable. I've enjoyed my association with STAR TREK and always have. It's been a very interesting, stimulating and intriguing 25 years. I hope we continue to be worthy of your admiration, and we all extend our heart felt thanks for your support."

MOONTRAP

Regarding his favorite episodes of the original TV series, these also often reflect how much his own character was utilized in those individual storylines as he selects "Spectre of the Gun," "I, Mudd," and "Trouble With Tribbles." "There are probably half a dozen episodes that I had real fun doing."

Has his notoriety associated with STAR TREK had a negative impact on him in any way?

"It hasn't had any negative affect on me personally. On the career? Well, in order to be able to say yes, it's impacted negatively on my career, one is asked to assume that had not STAR TREK been in my life, I would have had this totally enriching and rewarding career, and there is no guarantee that that would have happened. I think that my talents are comparable to those of most actors working in the industry, but I know wonderful performers who do little theater and pump gas. It is just as possible, or perhaps far more possible that I'd be out of the business than it would be that I would have had a rewarding career aside from STAR TREK."

Regarding the future, Koenig still hopes to one day appear in a sequel to the film MOONTRAP, a low budget science fiction film which had a limited theatrical release but was well received on cable and in the home video market. The producers of MOONTRAP are still trying to put together that sequel.

"There are people involved who are optimistic that it will get done. But I'm of the nature that I don't believe anything until they say, 'Roll 'em,' and then I'm not sure! It was a compliment to all involved that the picture was in BILLBOARD's top 40 for six weeks in a row. It sold 50,000 units at

$59.95. It was one of the happier experiences of my life. It would have been a happy experience even if the picture had been buried after two days. The atmosphere was great. People treated me very well. I did not abuse that treatment. We were like a family group. We shot it in Detroit. It was a small group. It was a union film—it was not a bootleg picture, which was important to me. I have only pleasant memories of that experience."

REMEMBERING RODDENBERRY

Walter also had some important observations to make about Gene Roddenberry, who passed away just a few short weeks before the release of STAR TREK VI: THE UNDISCOVERED COUNTRY.

"My association with Gene was generally very nice. He certainly was responsible for what's happened to me for the past 25 years. And no matter what isolated instances there were in which I felt frustrated by his behavior and angry at him, my very basic and overall feelings are one of gratitude toward him for involving me in what has happened all these years.

"He was a man who was always very warm. He always had time to say hello. Intransigent when it came to his own ideas, which is really a virtue because he could not be compromised, although he suffered for it early on, I think that ultimately it was one of the reasons why THE NEXT GENERATION is so much his vision because the studio knew that he could not be swayed.

Gene lost projects in the earlier days because of that obdurate posture, but THE NEXT GENERATION was really his vision undiluted. The good and the bad, it is his vision, and that must have been enormously satisfying to him because this is a business where there's a dozen cooks for every project. I admire that. I admire his integrity to his own beliefs."

CREATIVITY

Walter has been involved in many writing endeavors both in and out of STAR TREK. CHEKOV'S ENTERPRISE, his diary of working on STAR TREK: THE MOTION PICTURE (and which was reprinted in 1992) is only one of his books.

"The project I'm writing now has to do with a native American attorney and two white attorneys, a male and a female. It is about how their interaction with him affects all their lives. The actual plot itself was inspired by a real event. It had to do with the murder of a white person on a reservation and who would have jurisdiction over the proceedings. It was a fight between the tribal court, state court and the federal district court in the real case."

THE GRAND FAREWELL

Walter had positive feelings about ending the run with STAR TREK VI "I think it is a terrific way to go out. It's not a terrific way to go out for me because I had so little to do. But In terms of closure of this whole saga, I think it's a terrific film."

Had Walter tried to figure out ways to have a more prominent role in this closure or was it out of his hands?

"It probably wasn't out of my hands but I thought it was. I probably could have had meetings with Nick Meyer. He's a very bright man and very receptive to ideas. I did submit a treatment for STAR TREK VI when I thought the studio was going to be doing an academy days story, where they were going to be doing a flashback story using young actors playing the parts of Kirk and Spock, which was not really considered seriously for two reasons. One,

because at that particular moment they were totally committed to doing this other story, and two, I killed off five of the seven members of the cast. I left Kelley and Nimoy alive because there was reference to them in THE NEXT GENERATION. And when I saw the first draft of the script, I wrote some notes and sent them to Ralph Winter, who thought they had merit, and who sent them along to Nick.

"I possibly could have done something more with the character. Nick's a great guy and if I had a cogent argument he might have listened. But I just assumed that I couldn't make anything change, I couldn't make anything happen and I didn't."

GIVING CHEKOV HIS DUE

Walter isn't angry or embittered in any way. After all, he had some good scenes in STAR TREK II: THE WRATH OF KHAN and STAR TREK IV: THE VOYAGE HOME. This time it just happened to be somebody else's turn.

"Yes it was," he agreed. "It was somebody else's time, and if it couldn't be me, I'm glad that it was George. George really deserved it. George has been very professional about not complaining. He's threatened not to do a couple of the movies, but his public posture has always been one of being totally diplomatic about it and totally professional and he deserved the shot. As I say, that made it a little bit easier for me to digest. And also the fact that we had so many guest performers. There just wasn't the opportunity for everybody. So I never took it personally. I never felt that anybody was out to get me.

"I had a great time in STAR TREK IV. In fact if you had given me the amount of work I had in STAR TREK IV in each of the films, I'd be lobbying for seven, eight and nine right now. I know my position in the STAR TREK firmament. Nobody's ever going to shine the spotlight exclusively on my character, or even predominantly on my character. I don't think that what happened in IV was untoward or disproportionate to what I had to offer. It was well within my abilities and I think that kind of thing could have been done in every picture if a conscientious effort had been made."

[This chapter also includes material culled from a second interview with Walter Koenig conducted by Michael Ruff in July 1991.]

THE NURSE

Majel Barrett Roddenberry attending the wedding of Marina Sirtis on June 21, 1992.

CHAPTER 22

NURSE CHRISTINE CHAPEL

Christine Chapel has a unique beginning compared to all of the other crew members of the Enterprise. She is a genetically engineered humanoid, one of whose "twins" served on the Enterprise even before she did. Christine was "born" on Larmia VI. This Federation planet produces offspring in a non-sexual manner by combining the necessary genetic material taken from volunteers. At the Offspring Centers, technicians labor over fertilized cells to produce the finest human beings possible.

Kept in a growth solution where the cells are monitored, the fetus develops until it is ready to be transferred to a larger incubator. In the course of a year approximate 200 male and female offspring are brought into being in this manner.

Once they are "born," the children are ranked based on the genetic comparisons to their "siblings." Although some off-worlders regard this process as eugenics, the Larmians explain that, contrary to other genetic experiments, Larmian children who don't make top standards are not murdered, but instead treated with the same respect as the top ten percent "harvested" that year.

The offspring who would later choose to designate herself as Christine Chapel, ranked 27th out of that year's group of 200 children. Her lot number was 27, a fairly respectable rank. Her genetic sister was ranked Number One, a designation she chose to keep rather than assuming something as unnecessary as a "name." The sisters had been contrived from reproductive cells from the same elder Larmian volunteer. The two became friends but didn't spend a lot of time together as Number One received the separate intensive training required of those who ranked in the top ten.

Number Twenty-Seven was certainly a respectable rank, but it wasn't as accomplished nor as pure as those in the top ten. Both physically and mentally superb, Number Twenty-Seven's emotions weren't as rigidly controlled as those of Number One, which were made as stable as were humanly possible.

LIFE ON LARMIA

But genetic control of emotions was only achieved in a few, nor did the Larmians consciously pattern themselves after races such as the Vulcans. They were not unemotional. The Larmians looked upon forgetting emotion as not taking advantage of an asset, a tool. Emotions, to the Larmians, made people complete. And yet the Larmians did feel that controlled emotional responses were the most appropriate response to a situation. They accepted the positive characteristics of all shades of emotions. Larmians did their utmost to train their children to always behave appropriately.

Schooling for Larmians consisted of two levels: an indoctrination in facts and social training. Facts were learned while in a dream state. For instance, one dream would consist of memorizing and analyzing algebra equations. While another would consist of a chemistry experiment. This went on for ten years after they reached their fifth birthday.

Social training was an equally vital part of the training of the Larmian children. Number Twenty-Seven and other Larmian children spent their days experimenting in various real life social situations in which they discovered appropriate mental and emotional responses. During the non-training periods, the children were free to explore and experiment with what they had learned. For instance, social boundaries were learned under the watchful eyes of their elders. Children would steal each other's property and then have it stolen back from them.

Using these techniques, the children could analyze what was involved and what they learned from it. They would then take what they had learned and continuously apply it to the new lessons they were taught. In the case of stealing they were able to formulate an understanding that stealing was wrong.

Millions of different scenarios taught Larmian children everything, from the answers to large moral questions to such small, everyday matters as sharing a common bathroom. This is what Number Twenty-Seven experienced during her ten years of education growing up on Larmia VI.

BREAKING AWAY

Number Twenty-Seven finally left Larmia because she felt that it limited her. She longed to experience the spontaneous things in life. Until she was on the Enterprise, and until that day Spock was beginning to undergo pon farr and threw her out of his quarters, Number Twenty-Seven had never been yelled at for doing something inappropriate. She found the experience both frightening and exciting.

Because of her genetic make-up, Christine Chapel wasn't as perfect on certain unseen levels as Number One was. Her more emotional nature was just the more obvious manifestation of their differences. Number One was such good command material that she was the first officer on the Enterprise years before Christine even achieved a position which allowed her to be posted aboard that vessel. And by that time Number One had been promoted off the ship.

Number One was almost obsessive about being appropriate, and she could also fixate on a problem until it was resolved. This was precisely what Starfleet looked for in an officer. Number One would never change her name because it described her perfectly. It gave her that air of authority she wanted.

Unlike Christine, who didn't want to be "perfect," Number One idolized the Vulcan way and was surprised during her time aboard the Enterprise when she discovered that Spock was less Vulcan in his ways than she was. Number One believed that this was the reason she had achieved a higher rank than him. Years later she would encounter Spock again and discover that he had interpreted the Vulcan philosophy in ways she had never imagined could be so appropriately applied.

PERSONAL CHOICE

Christine changed her name because she wanted a means of identification which was more personal than a number. She became a nurse because she had emotions which made her want to care for people. These feelings also made her a curiosity on Larmia. She was certain that the name Christine would be more soothing to her patients than the number twenty-seven would be.

Upon graduation from nursing school, where Christine showed a particular aptitude (something which would no doubt have surprised Number One), Starfleet posted her as a staff nurse aboard the USS Exeter, which was leaving on a deep space mission. Her superior was a chief medical officer, Dr. Roger Korby. Korby was a brilliant physician and researcher, diving into the medical technology of every new culture the Exeter discovered, adding new knowledge to the Federation.

Christine admired Roger Korby but she soon found herself falling in love with him. Roger was dedicated and determined; alive with fire. Christine was attracted to the raw emotion that was so new to her. Initially Korby rebuffed her advances. But soon he realized that, with her Larmian training, she was a sensual woman possessed of great passion. He analyzed the significance of this and decided that becoming involved with Christine could be most instructive.

ALIEN MYSTIQUE

Roger continued his deep space exploration after becoming engaged to Christine, but on one of those missions he was reported lost. Korby had been part of a first contact landing party investigating an ancient culture in which the androids were slowly taking over. The Exeter continued searching for Korby, but without success.

Christine felt overwhelmed with loss. She had never experienced emotions like this before,

particularly to such an extreme. Tried as she might, she could not control the intensity of these emotions. Christine finally decided that perhaps Number One was not to be pitied so after all. This was a new form of pain which no medical journal had a cure for.

Returning to Earth, Christine tried to finish the research Roger had started. To her surprise Number One showed up and aided in helping her "sister" recover from her painful ordeal. Number One was now captain of the El Cid, a destroyer, and had requested shore leave for the first time in her fifteen year Starfleet career. Number One's somber reasoning reassured Christine that she was still sane and that life must go on.

When Christine transferred aboard the Enterprise as Chief Nurse, she found a vessel far more elaborate than the Exeter had been. Dr. McCoy was dedicated and adopted a pose of being an irascible country doctor who, although from Atlanta, had not been back to Earth for years. And then she met Spock, who could have been Number One's brother beneath the skin. Perhaps that is what attracted her to him, not that she would have ever considered doing anything inappropriate. To her Spock was an alien warrior, and only she could understand what he was really like. Perhaps one day he might even accept that truth from her.

CHAPTER 23

NURSING THE STARS: MAJEL BARRETT

Majel Lee Hudec was born in Cleveland, Ohio where she grew up. At the age of 10, her mother enrolled her in a workshop at the Cleveland Playhouse, which she found she loved. That love of acting would last life long. While attending Shaker Heights High School she continued to follow her interest in performing. But upon graduating from high school she attended college with the idea of studying to be a legal clerk. A career in acting seemed a bit far-fetched.

In Cleveland she majored in Theatre Arts at Flora Stone Mather College of Western Reserve University, which was a college exclusively for Women. It is now called Case University. From there she transferred to the University of Miami where she majored in Theatre Arts. It was at the University of Miami that she acquired her solid training in professional theater. During a school vacation at the time she did eleven weeks of summer stock stage acting in Bermuda.

Majel then attended law school for a year, but dropped out after receiving an "F" in a contract law course. This was clearly not for her. Then she relocated to New York City to pursue acting again and found that thousands of other people had the same idea, which made the competition for roles particularly fierce. Her initial acting work included the play "Models By Season," which was staged in Boston. It nearly made it to Broadway but closed out of town, as they say. Then she landed a nine-month stint in a road show tour of the play "The Solid Gold Cadillac." In this production she traveled to such cities as New Orleans, Austin, Oklahoma City and even San Francisco.

Then it was off to California to appear with Edward Everett Horton at the Pasadena Playhouse in the play "All for Mary." Majel continued to study acting with various teacher. While studying drama with Anthony Quinn, he was impressed with her talent to the degree that he helped her obtain work with Paramount Pictures. At Paramount in the late fifties she appeared in three films: BLACK ORCHID, AS YOUNG AS WE ARE and THE BUCCANEER. THE BUCCANEER also featured Quinn and was directed by the legendary Cecil B. DeMille.

But Majel wasn't satisfied doing films. In an interview in MEDIA WORLD MAGAZINE she stated, "Only the stars and director get anything worthwhile out of films. They get all the attention, the credit, the salary. They can afford to put a couple of months or more into one project. The support actors really just get a pat on the head with little to show for all the time spent. I saw what was happening in television and asked myself, why was I wasting my time with the movies?"

TV AND THE STARS

Majel appeared on THE WESTINGHOUSE DESILU PLAYHOUSE in 1959 in the episode "Christmas Surprise Package." She also appeared in such diverse television fare as WINDOW ON MAIN STREET ("The Charity Drive") and on PETE AND GLADYS, the old sitcom which starred Harry Morgan. One of the most popular shows on television in 1962 was BONANZA and Majel appeared on the episode "Gift of Water."

When she met Lucille Ball at an acting class being given by Sanford Meisner, the first lady of comedy liked what she saw in Majel and signed her to a contract at Desilu, the company she was now the sole owner of. Soon Majel appeared on an episode of THE LUCY SHOW ("Lucy Is A Kangaroo For A Day"), but the actress soon found that being under contract at a studio didn't mean they had you working all the time, and work is what she wanted to do.

By 1964 Majel was no longer under exclusive contract to Desilu and so she accepted a role on an episode of the new MGM series THE LIEUTENANT, which was produced by a young writer named Gene Roddenberry. Majel soon became friends with Gene, although they did not become romantically involved until his marriage broke up a couple of years later.

Also during 1964, Gene cast Majel in a major supporting role in "The Cage," which was the episode title of the first STAR TREK pilot. She played the second in command to Captain Pike on the Enterprise, and unlike the kinds of roles she was usually given, it was a strong female role. Certainly she was easily perceived as being on an equal footing with the starship commander himself. When NBC saw it they were put off by the idea of a woman in command and told Roddenberry to shoot another pilot and get rid of that woman named Number One.

In 1965 Majel continued landing parts and appeared in various episodes of such series as DR. KILDARE, 77 SUNSET STRIP, THE 11th HOUR and MANY HAPPY RETURNS. She even appeared on LEAVE IT TO BEAVER as the mother of Lumpy Rutherford. But invariably she played a secretary or a young mother, which weren't exactly the kinds of roles which gave an actress a lot to run with.

NURSE CHAPEL

Roddenberry sold STAR TREK to NBC after producing a second pilot. But he was so impressed with what Majel had done in "The Cage" that he hired her to appear in the series. Since she had used the name M. Leigh Hudec on the credits of the first STAR TREK pilot, Roddenberry hired her as Majel Barrett, gave her a blonde wig and NBC never knew that it was the same actress who had so disturbed them in "The Cage."

Chapel's character revealed that she was more than just Dr. McCoy's nurse in "The Naked Time" when she confessed her secret affection for Spock. This by-play did not emerge on the show again, though, until the second season premiere, "Amok Time. " In the opening scene of that episode, McCoy gently ribs Chapel about her infatuation with the Vulcan, whereupon she enters Spock's cabin and he nearly assaults her in an uncharacteristic fit of temper. We also see Christine Chapel's reaction when the Enterprise arrives at Vulcan and Spock reveals that T'Pring is his betrothed.

Although Chapel had a few featured roles on episodes now and then, most notably in the first season episode "What Are Little Girls Made Of?", she was largely kept in the background. One of the only two female regulars on STAR TREK, she was nonetheless seldom featured prominently in story-lines. Barrett was also the voice of the computer on the STAR TREK television series, a role she is repeating on STAR TREK—THE NEXT GENERATION as well. Her limited scenes on the show allowed her to appear in other projects, though.

In 1967 Majel appeared in the Walter Matthau film A GUIDE FOR THE MARRIED MAN. The movie was directed by one of Majel's favorite actors, Gene Kelly. Other TV shows she appeared in during the mid-sixties include THE WACKIEST SHIP IN THE ARMY, PLEASE DON'T EAT THE DAISIES and THE SECOND HUNDRED YEARS.

MRS. GENE RODDENBERRY

By the time STAR TREK was canceled in 1969, Majel Barrett and Gene Roddenberry had become an item. As soon as his divorce was final, Gene married Majel Barrett on August 6, 1969 in Tokyo, Japan. While scouting locations in Japan for an MGM project, Gene recalled, "I discovered I missed Majel a lot. Now, an American bachelor on an MGM expense account in Japan. . . this can be heaven. But I found myself with these pretty little girls in silk kimonos, talking to them about Majel. One night I realized what I was doing. I paid the girl, went back to my hotel and called up Majel to ask her if she would do me the honor of becoming my wife. We wanted to get married in Japan, but Majel didn't have a passport and was told it took a minimum of three days. Luckily, she's a good actress. She went down to the Federal Building, crying, 'I know him! The bastard won't wait that long!!' " She got her passport in twenty-four hours.

Gene felt that "it seemed sacrilegious to hire an American minister in Japan. Majel had to carry a dagger so she could kill herself if I dishonored her! She also had to carry a purse of coins so she could get home in case I changed my mind, and she had to wear a hat that hid the woman's horns of jealousy. All I had to do was carry a fan to keep cool." They were married in Tokyo, in a traditional Buddist-Shinto ceremony.

Gene had two daughters, Darleen and Dawn, from a previous marriage. Majel had three miscarriages before finally giving birth to a son, Eugene Wesley Roddenberry Jr., known as Rod, on February 5th, 1974. Rod didn't discover his parents were involved with STAR TREK until he was six, and later bought a SPACE: 1999 lunch box. Gene remarked once that he hoped his son would be a writer, but figured that Rod probably wouldn't just because it was what his dad wanted him to be.

A BUSY CAREER

Majel's other film credits include TRACK OF THUNDER, THE DOMINO PRINCIPLE, LOVE IN A GOLDFISH BOWL, THE QUICK AND THE DEAD,

SYLVIA and WESTWORLD. She has appeared in Gene Roddenberry's post-STAR TREK pilots GENESIS II, PLANET EARTH, SPECTRE and THE QUESTOR TAPES. Majel Barrett appeared as Sebastian's assistant, Lilith, in the opening and closing scenes of SPECTRE.

"My interest in doing this kind of story was partially brought about because my wife, Majel, is a passionate fan of horror films," Roddenberry stated, "and she had always wanted to play a witch. She did such a marvelous job that I'm sorry I didn't take her all the way through the film. Her performance was right on and certainly one of the more interesting characters."

Majel returned as Doctor Chapel in STAR TREK—THE MOTION PICTURE, but was then excluded from subsequent films until returning briefly in STAR TREK IV—THE VOYAGE HOME. Majel has never disguised her bitterness over this state of affairs. Even her return in THE VOYAGE HOME was marred by having most of her scenes left on the cutting room floor. Once Paramount took the STAR TREK movies away from Gene Roddenberry and turned them over to other producers, following the expensive problems encountered making STAR TREK—THE MOTION PICTURE, Majel Barrett was the only STAR TREK regular who did not return in all of the subsequent films. STAR TREK IV is the only other one she has appeared in since the first one.

A NEW PERSONA

But when Gene Roddenberry created STAR TREK—THE NEXT GENERATION, he also created a part for Majel. Lwaxana Troi is a far cry from the shrinking violet Christine Chapel. When Roddenberry created the character, he jokingly told his wife, "I've got a great part for you, and you don't even have to act." The implication being that the loud, overbearing Lwaxana is very similar to the true persona of Majel herself. Barrett has appeared on several episodes in the recurring role of the mother of Deanna Troi.

But just when we thought all her character would ever amount to is a cartoon, the episode "Half A Life" appeared in the fourth season. The teleplay by Peter Allan Fields has Lwaxana fall in love with an alien scientist who it turns out is about to reach the mandatory age of retirement. The problem is that on his world, when one reaches that age they are expected to commit ritual suicide. It's a touching, moving story which showed a more fully fleshed out character and revealed facets of Lwaxana never before hinted at. It remains one of the high points of the six years of THE NEXT GENERATION.

Majel Barrett continues to own and operate Lincoln Enterprises, a mail order business dealing in STAR TREK and other film related memorabilia. She still occasionally appears at STAR TREK conventions representing that business and selling official merchandise. Her off-screen hobbies include gold working, gem cutting and gourmet cooking, as well as golfing.

In October 1991, Majel was at her husband's side when he died following years of debilitating medical problems.

TALKING TO A SPACE NURSE

Majel Barrett first met Gene Roddenberry in the early sixties when she was going over to Screen Gems to interview for acting roles. She and Gene became friends for two or three years before she ever did STAR TREK. Majel worked on one of Gene's shows prior to STAR TREK when she appeared in an episode of THE LIEUTENANT, just as several other future members of the Enterprise crew had done. When Roddenberry worked with someone he liked, he remembered them for future projects. In fact she says that the part of Number One in the first STAR TREK pilot was actually written by Gene specifically with her in mind.

"They thought we were strange with this STAR TREK and this space talk, so they sent us out to Goldwyn Studios, which is an old, deserted place; there wasn't another thing shooting on the soundstage. I had to test Susan Oliver's makeup because she was too expensive and I was under contract already. I was cheap; they had to pay me anyway."

She also encountered someone there whom she would come to know very well in the years to come.

"There was another guy there by the name of Leonard Nimoy and Leonard became Spock. You'll notice that when you see 'The Menagerie,' that Leonard does smile, or has a little grin from time to time. My character was the one who was supposed to be very austere. We put this makeup on and Leonard tried the ears. Well, they didn't know what to do and the ears on Leonard stuck straight out. Not only that, but they wiggled when he talked."

IT'S NOT EASY BEING GREEN

The makeup tests they ran on Majel were very green and kept getting even more green as the test shots kept inexplicably failing. "But they kept on sending out the rushes and we would get it back the next day and there I was, just as pink and rosy as could possibly be. This went on for three days until finally they called the lab and said, 'What do we do? We're trying to get a green.' And they said, 'You want that? We've been color correcting!'"

But while they were in makeup they still had to eat lunch, and there was no commissary at the Goldwyn Studios.

"You had to walk out to the sidewalk, down the street and over to Washington Boulevard to go into a restaurant. And needless to say, Leonard (replete with experimental Vulcan ears) and I arm-in-armed it down the street. The cars honked, of course. The tooting, the stopping, the screeching and so forth. You expect that because even by Hollywood standards we looked strange. When we entered the restaurant the waitress automatically did a double-take, and the cast went into hysterical fits of laughter. We tried to ignore it, but the entire place was looking at us all the time. It's hard to eat like that.

"You know when someone is watching you, and you know how silly you look and how silly you feel. And here Leonard was looking at this green monster of some sort sitting across from him, and I was looking at this pointy-eared goblin, who—when he chews his food—his ears wiggle. Needless to say, we brown-bagged it from then on."

CLOSED DOORS

Later, after the second pilot had been filmed and STAR TREK had been picked up as a series, Barrett was back aboard as the nurse, only now the hijinks took place behind the scenes instead of on public streets.

"I remember John D.F. Black; the things we did to him were terrible. On his first day as story consultant on STAR TREK, Gene said to him, 'Look, I've got this actress coming in. I really don't have time to see her, so just talk to her for me.' He said, 'Well, what do I say?' And Gene said, 'I don't know, just put her off somehow or other.' John sat there and they sent me up. Now, I was prepared with this white bikini-type bathing suit on, and I went in and said, 'Mr. Black, I understand you are casting this movie and I really need. . . ' and all this time I'm taking my clothes off. Now this was John's first day on the job, and he sat there, his chair up against the second floor window—I thought he was going to fall out! He started saying, 'No! No! I don't want it to go this way!!'

"Well, everyone else was outside waiting for the proper moment to come in—which had gone past. I was down to nothing, practically. They finally opened up the door and said, 'John! What are you doing?!' At this point—the poor man—the telephone rings. It's his wife. She wants to know about his first day at work. I don't know if he'll ever forgive me."

When STAR TREK was canceled, Majel decided to involve herself in other things as well as acting.

As she told MEDIA WORLD magazine, "It wasn't that I was too typecast for other roles, like some of the STAR TREK people had been. I just wasn't as recognizable as Nurse Chapel, so that wasn't a hindrance when I was being considered for other parts. I just picked my acting jobs carefully, as I had plenty to do besides committing myself to TV shows and movies! I mean, I had a new husband to take care of, as well, so doing the Hollywood thing was obviously low on my list of priorities."

But she did enjoy her involvement with Filmation's animated STAR TREK cartoon series in 1974-75. "Doing a cartoon is the best kind of work an actor can get, especially when it's a great cartoon like the STAR TREK one. You can stumble in the studio, looking like hell, never put a bit of makeup or wardrobe on. Just grab some coffee, sit down and read your lines! It's great work if you can get it."

DR. CHAPEL

When STAR TREK returned as a motion picture in 1979, Majel Barrett was aboard with a promotion to Dr. Chapel. But the only STAR TREK film she appeared in thereafter was STAR TREK IV, and most of her part wound up on the cutting room floor. Initially she had a scene in THE VOYAGE HOME where she talks with Ambassador Sarek before he enters the council chambers. But in editing it was decided that it would be more dramatic to have Sarek make his entrance in the film directly into the council chamber without the preliminary scene. Thus Barrett's scene, and others, hit the cutting room floor.

But Barrett believes there have been other reasons why she is the only original cast member who hasn't appeared in every one of the movies.

"It might not be a good idea for Majel Barrett to go running around the set," she suggests, "not for Mrs. Gene Roddenberry. The movie series hasn't gotten past the point where they can handle the fact that Gene Roddenberry is the creator. It's just unfortunate." And so Majel has been largely sidelined in the motion pictures, but Gene managed to offset that injustice when he created THE NEXT GENERATION.

NEW VISION

Asked if she thinks something like STAR TREK would have been created by someone else if Gene hadn't crafted it, Majel is adamant in her observation. "No, definitely not. Everyone has tried and no one has succeeded in coming this close. Gene had things to say and they were comments that were universal. They were about war, love and peace; about everything that is universal. And no one has really come close to duplicating that in any other series or imitation."

When Gene Roddenberry was called upon to create a new version of STAR TREK with an entirely new cast, twenty years had passed since he'd originally created the first series and he wasn't exactly the same person he'd been then. In COMICS INTERVIEW magazine, Majel explained her husband's transformation.

"The television show was just simply that; it was 79 episodes of a television show made for commercial reasons—to sell soap. What it became, what happened afterwards, was Gene had changed his mind; his feelings. Remember, we had a lot of sex and violence and killing and things like that, and he didn't like that. He invented something that he hated afterwards! He hated the Klingons because he had painted them all bad, but there's no such thing as an all-bad race.

"So in the years after, when the reruns came on, he started going out and lecturing. He grew during that time and he changed his thinking, and each message that he left behind him said that there will be a tomorrow and tomorrow will be perfect! We will not have hate, and we will have diversity. His main thing, of course, was infinite diversity in infinite combinations; that was Gene's whole feeling about life, as a matter of fact. As he said, to be different is not necessarily to be ugly, and to have a different idea is not necessarily to be wrong, and the worst possible thing that could happen is if we were all to think and feel alike. If we can't enjoy the small variations that occur amongst people here on Earth, God help us if we get out into space and meet the large variations which are inevitably out there. This was his message and he grew with it."

And because of his expanded beliefs, when he brought the Klingons back he changed them. Originally the Klingons weren't going to be a part of THE NEXT GENERATION at all, but then he had an idea. . .

"He hated the Klingons so much; he hated the fact that he had created them, that he said he would not have any more Klingons around. But then he thought, 'Well, let's go one step further; let's have Klingons around but let's make them the good guys.' That's a much more true representation. So he corrected a lot of his mistakes, which he did consider very gross mistakes," Majel explained.

A CHARACTER WITH FLARE

During the first year of STAR TREK—THE NEXT GENERATION, Majel Barrett turned up in two roles. One was as the familiar voice for the ship's computer which she had done throughout the

original STAR TREK series in the '60s and which she duplicated exactly when doing the voice for the computer aboard the new Enterprise. On-screen she was seen in the episode "Haven" as Lwaxana Troi, the overbearing mother of ship's counselor Deanna Troi. She has reprised the character at least once in every season of THE NEXT GENERATION since then, except in season six where she instead appeared in an episode of DEEP SPACE NINE playing opposite Odo.

Majel has enjoyed playing Lwaxana Troi and has very specific ideas on who this woman is. "Lwaxana is sort of the Auntie Mame of the galaxy. She's a much more fun character and I can play her forever because I'm at an age where that's totally believable. I would like to continue to do that."

But why does STAR TREK keep going on? What keeps it so vital that not only to many of the old fans stick with it but the series continues to attract new fans as well?

"STAR TREK gave everyone a look into the future," she told STARLOG. ""It was such a positive thing which said, 'Yes, there is a tomorrow.' So many things that are happening today sort of point to the destruction of the entire world, let alone the entire universe. STAR TREK says there is a tomorrow and this is what it's going to look like."

AFTERWORDS

The following is a compilation of quotes from several books and magazines which show how a variety of authors viewed STAR TREK over the last two and a half decades, both before and after it was revived in 1979.

STAR TREK, STAR TREK— EVERYONE HAD AN OPINION

"Like Spain's Francisco Franco, STAR TREK has been fatally
dead for a long time. Now and then the mortuary shoots
an electric current through the corpse, and the resultant
spasm releases yet another manual or quiz or convention
or novel or book of fan fiction or what have you, but after
nearly a decade there's little life left in the old cadaver."

- Gil Lamont & James K. Burk
DeLAP'S F & SF REVIEW (March/April 1978)

The above quote seemed to reflect the feelings of a lot of people in science fiction fandom in the '70s regarding the increasing presence of STAR TREK fans at SF conventions and in SF in general. They obviously looked down on STAR TREK, and therefore chose to dismiss what they felt was a preponderance of interest in it. But what those intemperate remarks ignored is that STAR TREK, as well as other popular interests, have attained a life greater than that possessed by their phosphor dot TV image or the larger than life images projected on the silver screen. All of this is because it quite independently touched a common chord in many individuals. Some of these people, a large minority in fact, went through life for years quietly enamored with the series and unaware that they shared a common bond with countless strangers until the day they happened on a fanzine or walked into their first media convention and found themselves at a reunion of family they'd never known they had.

Before STAR TREK's return to the screen occurred with a fitful start in 1979's STAR TREK: THE MOTION PICTURE and its soaring sequel, THE WRATH OF KHAN, a groundswell of anti-STAR TREK backlash was developing. Most of it was generated by the attitude that "those people" were "invading" the otherwise sedate and pristine atmosphere of science fiction and comic book conventions. On the restroom wall at one San Diego Comic Con, someone with an artistic bent had done a large drawing of a woman copulating with a decaying Vulcan corpse and scrawled above it was the rallying cry: "Star Trek is dead."

As I write this I can't help but wonder how many times those erstwhile critics have seen all the new versions of STAR TREK which have come down the pike since 1979. How quickly passion does ebb and flow.

IT'S EVERYWHERE!
IT'S EVERYWHERE!

What these people seemed to be reacting to was the huge popularity of a TV show which had ceased to be in 1969. It was no longer new or even current, but was dead and gone. That seemed to be the objection. But how many of these same detractors read and collected novels by authors who were deceased? How many others read and reread the comic strips of artists who were dead or retired from the field? In both cases they were pursuing interests in things which to all intents and purposes were defunct with no hope of continuation by the talented people who originated them. But STAR TREK? Well, that's just a TV show that's in reruns. . . or so it seemed in 1978.

Just because something is in reruns (or reprints) does not mean that it cannot be studied and appreciated. The works of H.P. Lovecraft, Robert E. Howard, E.E. "Doc" Smith, Edgar Allan Poe, Clark Ashton Smith, Rod Serling, Edgar Rice Burroughs and many others including Wells and Verne are still read and enjoyed decades after their passing. Sir Arthur Conan Doyle died in 1930 but Sherlock Holmes is appreciated by more people today than ever before. Every year, it seems, someone is inspired to take pen in hand and create an "untold" tale of London's famous sleuth. Nicholas Meyer, the director of STAR TREK II and STAR TREK VI (and co-author of STAR TREK IV), wrote two best selling novels chronicling some strange tales of Baker Street's resident detective.

I raised some of these points when I wrote a letter commenting on the remarks quoted at the top of this article. I had hoped to receive some sort of reply or see the issue addressed in some manner befitting the stature of the magazine, but little did I know that I had witnessed the silent death throes of the publication. It faded away shortly thereafter, not unlike a mist which quietly dissipates at the first light of a morning sun, while the corpse of STAR TREK was resuscitated shortly thereafter and looks amazingly healthy these days.

THE MOST INFAMOUS REVIEW

No review of STAR TREK's coverage in the press, and the many observations and opinions it engendered, would be complete without first mentioning the infamous Cleveland Amory review of the series in the March 25, 1967 issue of TV GUIDE. This is the review that fans love to hate. Amory was TV GUIDE's resident critic in the sixties and he brought a style to his reviews which has been sorely lacking since he left the magazine in the early seventies. His pieces are highly entertaining to read even when he's panning a show you like. Amory was perhaps the first writer to comment on the incorrect use of English in the opening credo spoken by Captain Kirk each episode.

"The mission of the 'Star Ship' Enterprise is to seek out and discover new worlds - 'To boldly go,' as is stated each week, 'where no man has gone before.' In other words, Enterprise not only splits the infinite— but, horror of horrors, infinitives, too. And quite a trip this good ship has each week.

"The Enterprise has plenty of fun places to go, and, make no mistake about it, it has fun people to go to those fun places. First of all, there is Captain Kirk, who's pretty close to the last of the clean-cutters. When he says sternly, 'Affirmative' or 'Negative' to some scheming girl yeoman, you just know—well, he yeomeans it. Second, there is his space mate, Mr. Spock, a 'science officer' who not only has pointed ears but also, we are told, a 'precise, logical turn of mind (which he) inherited from his father, a native of the planet Vulcanis, who married an Earth woman.' (We've warned you men before about marrying below you.)"

This is not the only time the planet "Vulcanis" was mentioned in articles of that period. That's because the original publicity materials for the first year of STAR TREK referred to Mr. Spock's home planet as "Vulcanis," not Vulcan, but that was quickly changed. Even in "This Side Of Paradise," Spock is referred to as a "Vulcanian" for the first and only time.

Cleveland Amory's review concludes with the passage which most aroused the ire of the fans in those days. After describing Dr. McCoy's apparent demise from the lance of the Black Knight, Amory reconstructs what follows for his own ironic amusement.

" 'It's my fault!' cried yeoman Tonia Barrows (Emily Banks), who had hallucinated up both Don Juan and the Black Knight. 'I'm to blame!' But Captain Kirk shook her. 'I need every crewman alert,' he said. 'Face front. Don't talk. Don't think. Don't breathe!' It was good advice—and in our opinion the best way for an adult to watch this show. For the kids, though, let 'em breathe. Let 'em even hallucinate. They'll love it."

PANNED AND PRAISED

Even the trade paper DAILY VARIETY insisted the series wouldn't work. Their published review in the September 14, 1966 issue read in part: "STAR TREK obviously solicits all out suspension of disbelief, but it won't work. Even within its sci-fi frame of reference it was an incredible and dreary mess of confusion and complexities at the kickoff. The interplanetary spaceship trudged on for a long hour with hardly any relief from violence, killings, hypnotic stuff and a distasteful, ugly monster." And if that wasn't bad enough, the review went on to say, "By a generous stretch of the imagination, it could lure a small coterie of the smallfry, though not happily time slotted in that direction. It's better suited to the Saturday morning kidvid bloc."

It was a depressing day on the Desilu lot when that review appeared, and that was after just one episode. If only hardcore science fiction fans were capable of understanding the show, while the average person was left perplexed (like the VARIETY reviewer certainly was), Roddenberry had to have wondered whether the show would even last through a single season.

But VARIETY took another shot at the show two years later, and inexplicably liked it much better when reviewing one of its worst episodes! In the September 25, 1968 issue, the review opened by stating: "STAR TREK has drifted far demographically since its days as kid fare and has now made the transition complete with a move into the late hours. It retains its vigor and spatial spookiness, although its chief characters are largely caricatures and the dialogue tends to turgidity. However, for males of all ages at least, it also retains a bevy of shapely femmes in tight and revealing space suits and enough conflict to accommodate the action-happy."

If the series were really no more than the review stated, NBC never would have canceled it since this reviewer describes exactly the kind of show the networks love to put on the air! What the VARIETY reviewer really liked about STAR TREK says more about the state of TV at that time than anything else could: "The best part of the show continues to be the sets and special effects, an impressive array of blinking and beeping gadgets." This very attitude encapsulated exactly what Roddenberry hated about some people's perceptions of science fiction.

AN EARLY LOOK BACK

And then there's John Baxter's review of the TV series in SCIENCE FICTION IN THE CINEMA (Paperback Library, 1970), one of the first reviews of STAR TREK looking back after its cancellation.

". . .STAR TREK (1968), after beginning well with a cleverly constructed double episode called MENAGERIE, degenerated sharply into stock situations. MENAGERIE is an interesting example of prudent TV production. Originally made as THE CAGE, a one-hour pilot for the series, it starred Jeffrey Hunter as the captain of a space battleship who rescues castaway Susan Oliver from telepathic aliens on a dying world. By the time the series had been accepted. Hunter was no longer available, so the producers incorporated the original hour into a two hour program in which William Shatner, the series' original star, investigates the circumstances of Hunters landing, with Hunter, a disfigured and unrecognizable victim of a space accident, beside him on the ship. The first program was viewed in segments as a flashback, some extra action added to tie up loose ends. On the whole an extremely clever piece of reorganization.

"Like so many other series, STAR TREK became caught in a profitable groove, in its case the idea of worlds in which societies had developed parallel with earth. This preoccupation began with TOMORROW IS YESTERDAY, an early episode in which Shatner's future starship is sent back in time, landing on the Earth of the sixties. Presumably intoxicated by the ease of doing an SF show in stock sets and with formula situations, the producers soon offered a planet like Nazi Germany, another like Chicago in the thirties. A third story was nothing but a space version of a wartime submarine drama, two space ships hunting each other with sophisticated versions of sonar. Marginally interesting as esoterica, none of these programs deserve serious consideration as SF.

"An exception, however, was an episode called CHARLIE X, directed by Lawrence Dobkin with Robert Walker Jr. as a telepath which the starship Enterprise unwittingly picks up. Adolescent and vindictive, the boy slips from puppy love to childish hatred in a moment, while the crew's reactions convey perfectly the terror of men faced with a power impossible to fight. Walker's acting is superb, an animal contortion of his face horribly suggesting the blast of hate that destroys those who oppose him. With it he melts the pieces of a three-dimensional chess set on which he has lost the game, and later, being angered by the laughter of some crewman, stops them abruptly. Seen first only as shadows, a girl gropes around the corner of a corridor to reveal her face changed to a smooth mask of flesh. Shape means nothing in his world, and when he changes a girl into a scuttling lizard we imagine when he advances on another with his hand behind his back and the coy offer of 'something for her' that it is this creature he will flourish in her face. But his hand holds instead a rose. Horror too can have its poetry, evil its own special beauty."

OVERLOOKING THE OBVIOUS

John Baxter devotes three whole paragraphs to STAR TREK and although two of the three are fairly generous in their praise, it ultimately presents a myopic view of the series as a whole which would make anyone who had never seen it wonder what all the shouting was about. He praises "The Menagerie" but drop-kicks the show for doing episodes using stock sets with formula situations, singling out "Patterns of Force" (Nazi Germany) and "A Piece of the Action" (Chicago in the thirties), both second season shows, while ignoring such key episodes as "City On The Edge Of Forever," "This Side Of Paradise," "Mirror, Mirror" and others which are far more representative of what STAR TREK was trying to accomplish in its setting with continuing characters.

While Baxter does single out "Charlie X" for praise, he never mentions the obvious inspiration that episode owes to a certain 1961 novel titled STRANGER IN A STRANGE LAND, about a human child raised on Mars who learned fantastic powers (such as making things go away) from non-corporeal beings. One of the last things Charlie says in the episode when he's pleading to stay is that the creatures that raised him don't even have real bodies that he can touch.

But Baxter's biggest oversight is that he makes no mention whatsoever of the characters. Granted, what initially hooked me on the series were episodes like "Where No Man Has Gone Before" and "This Side of Paradise," but it didn't take long to realize that they were doing something different with their continuing characters. They weren't interchangeable. They seemed to not only care about what was transpiring around them but about each other as well, and this above all else is what has made the series endure. Fifteen years before HILL STREET BLUES and half a decade before MASH, this show presented an ensemble of characters who attained levels of interest equal to the finest moments in those later shows.

William Shatner was the supposed star, but without the other actors for him to play off of, the effect would not have been the same. Mr. Spock, who began as a secondary character, so fascinated the viewing audience that they demanded to see more of him and he quickly attained the level of importance equal with Kirk, and this duo has symbolized STAR TREK ever since. Only someone who never watched enough episodes to notice that something was going on between these people could have possibly overlooked mentioning them in some capacity beyond the function they fulfilled in the series. It's like seeing one episode and judging the other seventy-eight from that, or reading one story by a writer and figuring that all the rest must be exactly the same.

THE GOOD DOCTOR

One of the early supporters of STAR TREK was noted author Isaac Asimov, who from time to time contributed articles to TV GUIDE commenting on the state of imaginative television fare as he saw it. He had a few words to say about the early days of the STAR TREK phenomenon in the April 29, 1967 issue of TV GUIDE in an article with the unfortunate title, "Mr. Spock Is Dreamy."

Said Asimov, "A revolution of incalculable importance may be sweeping America, thanks to television. And thanks particularly to STAR TREK, which in its noble and successful effort to present good science fiction to the American public, has also presented everyone with an astonishing revelation."

That revelation comes about when Asimov's daughter remarks that "I think Mr. Spock is dreamy!" because he's so smart.

"And then, then, came this blinding revelation. Here I had been watching STAR TREK since its inception because I like it, because it is well-done, because it is exciting, because it says things (subtly and neatly) that are difficult to say in 'straight' drama and because science fiction, properly presented, is the type of literature most appropriate to our generation.

"But it hadn't occurred to me that Mr. Spock was sexy. I had never realized that such a thing was possible; that girls palpitate over the way one eyebrow goes up a fraction; that they squeal with passion when a little smile quirks his lip. And all because he's smart!

"If I had only known! If I had only known!

"But I am spreading the word now. It may be far too late for me (well, almost), but there is a new generation to consider!

"Men! Men everywhere! Don't listen to the lies! I have learned the secret at last. It is sexy to be smart!"

THE FUTURE THAT NEVER WAS

In the Fall Preview Issue of TV GUIDE for the '68-'69 season, the listing for STAR TREK's return had some interesting information.

"More hazardous than all their encounters in outer space for the Star Trekkers are those Nielsen ratings, and they just barely eked by with a renewal for this season. Last term, their future was in considerable doubt, and only a heavy mail campaign from avid viewers played an important part in keeping the show on.

"Executive producer Gene Roddenberry still was on the verge of quitting the show because they changed its time slot to 10 p.m. Fridays, a time he still thinks bodes no good for the future of his series, since it slots the show opposite the movies on CBS and JUDD on ABC. But he did agree to remain with it, despite his unhappiness at the change.

"Roddenberry tells us that this season the only change is to expose the secondary characters more fully, to give viewers a better idea of their personalities. He remarks of the gang in Trek, 'We have the truly multi-racial cast, and in two years we've had only three crank letters.' In one of the stories this season, the Trekkers land on a planet identical in physical makeup to earth. On that planet, the police are selected as carefully as we select scientists, and the question is posed: Could our police be better? 'We are using science fiction to show the police as they could or should be if they had support from the public, and scientific support,' explains ex-cop Roddenberry."

Gene Roddenberry did, of course, finally step down from active participation in the third season of STAR TREK and the result was obvious. One of those obvious results is that the story described above was never filmed. Suggested 25 years ago, that particular plot would be just as timely were it presented today, and fact it would seem to be inspired by today's headlines rather than by the musings of an ex-policeman in the 1960s.

THE FUTURE CHANGES. . .

Frederick Pohl also had something to say about STAR TREK in his non-fiction book THE WAY THE FUTURE WAS (Ballantine Books, 1978).

". . .This is now diagnosable as the STAR TREK syndrome. As science fiction goes, STAR TREK isn't much. There's not a fresh idea in all the three years of it put together, nothing that has not been done before, and is usually much better in the pages of some science fiction magazine or book. But the people who saw STAR TREK numbered forty million. The overwhelming majority of them had never been exposed to anything like it before. They had never really thought about the possibility of life on other planets, or time travel, or what it would be like to cruise through space, or how societies might resemble (or differ from) our own, until they caught it on the boob tube, and to them it was Revelation. To them. To us, decades earlier. Above all, to me."

It was fashionable among some circles of science fiction writers to bash STAR TREK in the '70s. In the '80s many had flip-flopped on their views.

For instance, Frederick Pohl's opinion of STAR TREK seemed to change from the quote above first published in 1978 to this next one taken from SCIENCE FICTION STUDIES ON FILM by Frederick Pohl and Frederick Pohl IV (Ace Books, 1981).

". . . A feature film? Good idea; so Paramount started preparing scripts and lining up talent. The talent was coy. Shatner, Nimoy and all the others had been convinced of their godhood by tens of thousands of Trekkies at dozens of conventions, and each one expected to see that reflected in a pay check. A script was also elusive. First shot went to Roddenberry himself, who created a sort of 'generations' story of the old age of the crew, coming back for one last go at the bad guys. Paramount nixed it and went on. It all took time, but as months passed they had a script at last. Philip Kaufman was signed to direct what he called 'essentially a Leonard Nimoy Spock story. . . it was a love story and it was adult science fiction' when the ax fell.

". . . The fourth network dream died hard, but at last it died and Paramount made its bet. It would be a feature film. Only question was, what would the film be? Roddenberry wrote the script, and the Paramount people vetoed it. They hired Robert Silverberg to write one, and vetoed that too. At least a dozen writers of one kind or another were put on the payroll for long periods or short to try and come up with the magic idea that would make it all come together. But none of the writers could please; and at last Paramount remembered the scripts it had commissioned for the 'Fourth Network ' series. It reached back in among them and pulled out the Alan Dean Foster story that had been intended as a lead off. And that became STAR TREK—THE MOTION PIC-TURE. Viewers who think that TMP seems rather like any random episode from the television series have exactly the right of it.

"There exists a novel version of the script, written be Gene Roddenberry, which shows a lot of inventiveness and interesting detail. Very little of it appears in the film. It is not likely that Roddenberry chose to eliminate the scenes, or that Paramount refused to foot the bill. The explanation is almost certainly that the special effects fiasco which almost doomed the film caused them to be dropped, for at almost the last minute

Paramount switched special effects studios and turned everything over to Douglas Trumbull when the original contractor failed to deliver.

"STAR TREK, THE MOTION PICTURE represents Hollywood at its lunatic worst. What appeared on the screen was no more than a rescue operation, the best compromise that could be reached between what Roddenberry wanted and what cold reality allowed. And yet-what a pleasure to see them together again!" [Italics mine.]

STAR TREK VS. STAR WARS

In THE WORLD OF SCIENCE FICTION (Ballantine Books, 1979), science fiction author Lester Del Ray had this to say:

". . . Yet I remember that STAR TREK was supposed to have some vast effect on the circulation of science fiction. Probably it had some but not much. And when Sputnik went up, everyone was convinced that the age of science fiction had begun—after which the circulation of the magazines continued to fall slightly.

"Obviously, only time will provide the answers. But in my opinion, STAR WARS is going to have a very strong effect on the continued success of science fiction.

"I discount results of STAR TREK from my experience with the followers of that television program. By and large, the audience that watched those programs did not become fans of science fiction, though there was considerable science fiction used. They became primarily fans of Mr. Spock, the long-eared Vulcan member of the crew, as played by Leonard Nimoy —and to a lesser extent of the rest of the crew. It was much more like other fandoms than like the fandom of science fiction. Many, in fact, acted as if they believed in the literal truth of what they saw, and most seemed to take the program far too seriously to dabble around with anything else in science fiction. . .

". . . But STAR WARS has a different impact. To begin with, of course, it is science fiction from start to finish. It takes robots, its aliens, its star travel and everything else very much for granted, just as science fiction learned to do. (George Lucas, unlike most Hollywood directors, seems to have an excellent familiarity with science fiction.) The characters are not the basic center of interest—rather the whole movie is.

"Furthermore, there is a much stronger tie-in with paperback science fiction. Ballantine/Del Rey Books is bringing out a series of 'spin-off' novels, each dealing with some of the characters of the movie. These will be by established science fiction authors. It is hoped that readers who buy such books will be led to other works by those same authors, thus moving them from STAR WARS to general science fiction. The first of all these books, SPLINTER OF THE MINDS EYE by Alan Dean Foster, has already been released, and preliminary reports following a healthy sale indicate that Foster's other books are beginning to sell more rapidly.

"In the case of STAR TREK, the original novelizations were done by James Blish, a highly regarded writer; but when the young fans of the series tried his other books, they must have found them totally beyond their age level. There was little cross-movement into science fiction."

Lester Del Rey was up front in pointing out that his company was issuing new STAR WARS books, but in fact his observations about STAR TREK fans were not just all too often true, but they were just as true of STAR WARS fans. Media fans, by and large, tend to become fans only of the books inspired by the media they are fans of. When STAR WARS faded in the mid-eighties, the media fans just turned their attention to something else, but by and large that attention was not drawn to the general science fiction book rack. The reason there are more STAR TREK novels being published now than ever before is that the STAR TREK fans who by the books prefer to read only STAR TREK books. Only a small percentage allow their attention to wander over to what else is on the shelf nearby. Don't ask me to explain why; it's just the truth.

SCIENTIFIC OBSERVATIONS

Writer Jerry Pournell found himself having to defend a character he created in A MOTE IN GOD'S EYE (with Larry Niven, Ace Books, 1979) because it seemed to bear more than just a passing resemblance to a character on the ubiquitous STAR TREK.

". . . We chose the Chief Engineer, largely because in the contemporary world it is a fact that a vastly disproportionate number of ships engineers are Scots, and that seemed a reasonable thing to project into the future.

"Alas, some critics have resented that, and a few have accused us of stealing Mr. Sinclair from STAR TREK. We didn't. Mr Sinclair is what he is for perfectly sound astrographical reasons."

Carl Sagan, who has done as much to bring science to the people and demystify it for most of us as anyone has, had an interesting observation to make about STAR TREK in his book BROCA'S BRAIN (Random House,1974) .

". . . I have the same trouble with STAR TREK, which I know has a wide following and which some thoughtful friends tell me I should view allegorically and not literally. But when astronauts from Earth set down on some far distant planet and find the human beings there in the midst of a conflict between two nuclear super powers, which call themselves the Yangs and the Coms, or their phonetic equivalents, the suspension of disbelief crumbles. In a global terrestrial society centuries in the future, the ship's officers are embarrassingly Anglo-American. Only two of twelve or fifteen interstellar vessels are given non-English names, Kongo and Potemkin. (Potemkin and not Aurora?)

"And the idea of a successful cross between a 'Vulcan' and a terrestrial simply ignores what we know of molecular biology. (As I have remarked elsewhere, such a cross is about as likely as the successful mating of a man and a petunia.) According to Harlan Ellison, even such sedate biological novelties as Mr. Spock's pointy ears and permanently querulous eyebrows were considered by network executives far too daring; such enormous differences between Vulcans and humans would only confuse the audience, they thought, and a move was made to have all physiologically distinguishing Vulcan features effaced."

ACROSS THE CHANNEL

Brian Aldiss, a fine British SF writer, managed to watch one STAR TREK episode and then reviewed the entire series in DREAM MAKERS (1980, edited by Charles Platt) when he said, ". . . the negative side is that the media have a great grip in the States, and so you get hogwash like STAR TREK, with its bright—well, it's not very bright, actually—this tinsel view of the future, and the galaxy, which has to be optimistic. I did once manage to see an episode all the way through, and at the end Captain Kirk says to the—the chap with the ears—'Well, this proves that the galaxy's too small for white men and green men to fight one another,' and

Spock nods and says, 'That's right,' and they clap each other on the shoulder, and up comes the music. Well, what Spock should have said was, 'Why the fuck shouldn't white men and green men fight together? Of course there's plenty of room.' Liberal platitudes do distress me.

      "And yet I remember having this argument with some quite high-powered chaps, and they said, 'That's a very subversive point of view, you may think these are platitudes, but they actually do a lot of good.' But I still think that science fiction should be subversive, it shouldn't be in the game of consolations, it should shake people up. I suppose because that's what it did to me when I started reading it, and that was valuable. It should question things. I have to say, I owe a lot to John W. Campbell and his damned editorials in ANALOG. I believe that you should challenge everything, you know? Occasionally, in my more manic moods, I still carry that early Campbell banner: Science Fiction should tell you things you don't want to know."

      It's unfortunate that Aldiss based his opinion of STAR TREK solely on an episode like "Arena" or "Let That Be Your Last Battlefield," but he does raise an interesting point. STAR TREK was certainly never subversive or dangerous in the views it purveyed, however much one wants to point to something like "A Taste of Armageddon" with its heavily disguised comments on the Vietnam war. The closest STAR TREK ever came to being subversive was in the third season when "The Enterprise Incident" was conceived as a take-off on the Pueblo Incident and was originally supposed to have concluded with Kirk questioning the ethics of his espionage mission behind Romulan lines, and whether spying is ever morally justified. Even as we cruise through the '90s, STAR TREK: THE NEXT GENERATION stays on the same safe path blazed by its '60s ancestor.

      But there have been glimmers which indicate that the current producers do recognize the subversive potential in science fiction. In season 5 of THE NEXT GENERATION the episode "The Outcast" certainly bothered some people, and in STAR TREK—DEEP SPACE NINE the first season episode "Duet" presented a dramatic character study dealing with the horrors of internment camps which presented some of the finest writing and acting in the 27 year history of the STAR TREK phenomenon.

      So STAR TREK is more than what those casual critics who only view it from afar have given it credit for. It has accomplished a lot more since 1966 than they seem to realize.

THE HISTORY OF TREK

James Van Hise

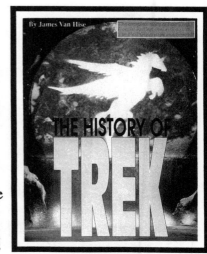

The complete story of Star Trek from Original conception to its effects on millions of Lives across the world. This book celebrates the 25th anniversary of the first "Star Trek" television episode and traces the history of the show that has become an enduring legend—even the non-Trekkies can quote specific lines and characters from the original television series. The History of Trek chronicles "Star Trek" from its start in 1966 to its cancellation in 1969; discusses the lean years when "Star Trek" wasn't shown on television but legions of die hard fans kept interest in it still alive; covers the sequence of five successful movies (and includes the upcoming sixth one); and reviews "The Next Generation" television series, now entering its sixth season. Complete with Photographs, The History of Trek reveals the origins of the first series in interviews with the original cast and creative staff. It also takes readers behind the scenes of all six Star Trek movies, offers a wealth of Star Trek Trivia, and speculates on what the future may hold.

$14.95.....160 Pages
ISBN # 1-55698-309-3

THE MAN BETWEEN THE EARS:
STAR TREKS LEONARD NIMOY

James Van Hise

Based on his numerous interviews with Leonard Nimoy, Van Hise tells the story of the man as well as the entertainer.

This book chronicles the many talents of Leonard Nimoy from the beginning of his career in Boston to his latest starring work in the movie, Never Forget. His 25-year association with Star Trek is the centerpiece, but his work outside the Starship Enterprise is also covered, from such early efforts as Zombies of the Stratosphere to his latest directorial and acting work, and his stage debut in Vermont.

$14.95.....160 Pages
ISBN # 1-55698-304-2

COUCH POTATO INC.   5715 N. Balsam Rd   Las Vegas, NV 89130   (702)658-2090

Use Your Credit Card 24 HRS — Order toll Free From: **(800)444-2524** Ext 67

TREK: THE MAKING OF THE MOVIES
James Van Hise

TREK: THE MAKING OF THE MOVIES tells the complete story both on-screen and behind the scenes of the biggest STAR TREK adventures of all. Plus the story of the STAR TREK II that never happened and the aborted STAR TREK VI: STARFLEET ACADEMY.

$14.95.....160 Pages
ISBN # 1-55698-313-1

TREK: THE LOST YEARS
Edward Gross

The tumultouos, behind-the-scenes saga of this modern day myth between the cancellation of the original series in 1969 and the announcement of the first movie ten years later. In addition, the text explores the scripts and treatments written throughout the 1970's, including every proposed theatrical feature and an episode guide for STAR TREK II, with comments from the writers whose efforts would ultimately never reach the screen.

This volume came together after years of research, wherein the author interviewed a wide variety of people involved with every aborted attempt at revival, from story editors to production designers to David Gautreaux, the actor signed to replace Leonard Nimoy; and had access to exclusive resource material, including memos and correspondences, as well as teleplays and script outlines.

$12.95.....132 Pages
ISBN # 1-55698-220-8

COUCH POTATO INC.   5715 N. Balsam Rd   Las Vegas, NV 89130   (702)658-2090

Use Your Credit Card 24 HRS — Order toll Free From: **(800)444-2524** Ext 67

BORING, BUT NECESSARY ORDERING INFORMATION

Payment:

Use our new 800 # and pay with your credit card or send check or money order directly to our address. All payments must be made in U.S. funds and please do not send cash.

Shipping:

We offer several methods of shipment. Sometimes a book can be delayed if we are temporarily out of stock. You should note whether you prefer us to ship the book as soon as available, send you a merchandise credit good for other goodies, or send your money back immediately.

Normal Post Office: $3.75 for the first book and $1.50 for each additional book. These orders are filled as quickly as possible. Shipments normally take 5 to 10 days, but allow up to 12 weeks for delivery.

Special UPS 2 Day Blue Label Service or Priority Mail: Special service is available for desperate Couch Potatoes. These books are shipped within 24 hours of when we receive the order and normally take 2 to 3 three days to get to you. The cost is $10.00 for the first book and $4.00 each additional book .

Overnight Rush Service: $20.00 for the first book and $10.00 each additional book.

U.s. Priority Mail: $6.00 for the first book and $3.00.each additional book.

Canada And Mexico: $5.00 for the first book and $3.00 each additional book.

Foreign: $6.00 for the first book and $3.00 each additional book.

Please list alternatives when available and please state if you would like a refund or for us to backorder an item if it is not in stock.

COUCH POTATO INC.   5715 N. Balsam Rd   Las Vegas, NV 89130   (702)658-2090

Use Your Credit Card 24 HRS — Order toll Free From: **(800)444-2524** Ext 67

ORDER FORM

_____ Trek Crew Book $9.95
_____ Best Of Enterprise Incidents $9.95
_____ Trek Fans Handbook $9.95
_____ Trek: The Next Generation $14.95
_____ The Man Who Created Star Trek: $12.95
_____ 25th Anniversary Trek Tribute $14.95
_____ History Of Trek $14.95
_____ The Man Between The Ears $14.95
_____ Trek: The Making Of The Movies $14.95
_____ Trek: The Lost Years $12.95
_____ Trek: The Unauthorized Next Generation $14.95
_____ New Trek Encyclopedia $19.95
_____ Making A Quantum Leap $14.95
_____ The Unofficial Tale Of Beauty And The Beast $14.95
_____ Complete Lost In Space $19.95
_____ ..doctor Who Encyclopedia: Baker $19.95
_____ Lost In Space Tribute Book $14.95
_____ Lost In Space With Irwin Allen $14.95
_____ Doctor Who: Baker Years $19.95
_____ Doctor Who: Pertwee Years $19.95
_____ Batmania Ii $14.95
_____ The Green Hornet $14.95 _____ Special Edition $16.95

_____ Number Six: The Prisoner Book $14.95
_____ Gerry Anderson: Supermarionation $17.95
_____ Addams Family Revealed $14.95
_____ Bloodsucker: Vampires At The Movies $14.95
_____ Dark Shadows Tribute $14.95
_____ Monsterland Fear Book $14.95
_____ The Films Of Elvis $14.95
_____ The Woody Allen Encyclopedia $14.95
_____ Paul Mccartney: 20 Years On His Own $9.95
_____ Yesterday: My Life With The Beatles $14.95
_____ Fab Films Of The Beatles $14.95
_____ 40 Years At Night: The Tonight Show $14.95
_____ Exposing Northern Exposure $14.95
_____ The La Lawbook $14.95
_____ Cheers: Where Everybody Knows Your Name $14.95
_____ SNL! The World Of Saturday Night Live $14.95
_____ The Rockford Phile $14.95
_____ Encyclopedia Of Cartoon Superstars $14.95
_____ How To Create Animation $14.95
_____ How To Draw Art For Comic Books $14.95
_____ King And Barker:an Illustrated Guide $14.95
_____ King And Barker: An Illustrated Guide II $14.95

100% Satisfaction Guaranteed.

We value your support. You will receive a full refund as long as the copy of the book you are not happy with is received back by us in reasonable condition. No questions asked, except we would like to know how we failed you. Refunds and credits are given as soon as we receive back the item you do not want.

NAME:_____

STREET:_____

CITY:_____

STATE:_____

ZIP:_____

TOTAL:_____ SHIPPING_____

SEND TO: Pioneer Books, Inc. 5715 N. Balsam Rd., Las Vegas, NV 89130